More Praise for "Masterminds Unleashed: Selling for Geniuses"

"Let's face it. We're *all* salespeople, whether it's our direct responsibility or not in our organizations. The question is: are you *comfortable* being a salesperson? The next is: are you *effective* at sales? If you answered "no" to either of those questions, this book is meant just for you – it gives you a simple, easy to follow, step-by-step approach to making sales happen. This is a fantastic group of authors, who are all master salespeople in their own right – definitely a worthwhile read."

—**Adam J. Kovitz**, CEO, Founder & Publisher, The National Networker

"Sales is a profession where only a few practitioners receive the lion's share of the reward. Learn how to be one of those few by reading and applying the principles and techniques in this slim volume. The good news is there is a proven way to success, and more good news is it is not easy. Be one of those who undertakes the exacting commitment and discipline to be the lion in your company's sales department."

—**Joel Anderson**, CEO and President, International Warehouse Logistics Association

"*Selling for Geniuses* is an excellent compilation of advice on how to improve your business development skills. If you are a lone entrepreneur or small business owner without a formal sales background, you will find the information in this book practical, accessible and immediately useful. I highly recommend it!"

—**Greg Williams**, Executive Vice President, Glaser Technology, Inc.

"Dan Paulson has guided me in growing 32% the first year and we are still growing. I am having more fun in my business than I ever had before. This coaching relationship has given me the confidence to build a facility, which I own, that is eight times larger than what I was working out of before the relationship. Much of the growth we have seen involved building customer loyalty and strengthening our sales. Our referral business is now over 70%! *Selling for Geniuses* is a great resource and I strongly recommend it for my colleagues and associates."

—**Dr. David Ducommun**, DDS. Madison No Fear Dentistry

"I've known Rick Kolster for over 30 years. Character, Integrity, Drive, Passion and Work Ethic are just a few of the words that describe Coach Rick best. He's been a salesman, yet he's never had to sell a thing. His selling tool is his passion and he teaches it to you. Being a speaker myself for over 10 years I have found that many of the inspirational speakers out there don't "walk the walk." *Coach Rick Walks the Talk*. He's passionate about what he's says because he really believes it and that's *powerful*."

—**Diamond Dallas Page**

"Masterminds Unleashed" gives practical advice that the reader can put to use immediately. There are great tips on how to make yourself visible within your community and among potential buyers, in person and on the internet. We've adopted the four point system and gained positive results in the first week!"

—**John J. Zevalkink**, President and CEO, Columbian Logistics Network

Masterminds

UNLEASHED

Selling
for
GENIUSES

*Selling When Selling
Isn't in Your Title*

Scholz • Boykin • Greisen • Kolster
Lunquist • Nielsen • Paulson • Smith

ISBN-13   978-1-60013-400-5
           1-60013-400-9

Published by...
INSIGHT PUBLISHING
647 Wall Street
Sevierville, Tennessee 37862

Printed in the United States of America

10 9 8 7 6 5 4 3 2 1

Table of Contents

Foreword

PERHAPS THIS DESCRIBES YOU. You are an aging boomer or a mid-career professional. You have had a long career with a couple of different large companies, steadily climbing the corporate ladder. Maybe you had a few slips along the way. You have a mortgage, a family and a few dollars in investments. Not enough to retire on, but an okay sum. Life is good.

You are actively engaged in playing the big company game, a little fat, dumb and happy. Four weeks of vacation, a great 401K, stock options...and then the word starts filtering through the ranks that your company is restructuring ...again! Change is good, you think to yourself. You call your boss and ask who you are going to be reporting to this week.

He responds, "No one. You are getting the package."

Packages were always supposed to be a good thing, right? They are especially good when they are brightly wrapped under the Christmas tree or given on a birthday. However when the words "you are getting the package" are aimed at you, those words take on a whole new meaning.

Perhaps the words "Thank God" slip from your lips. Perhaps the words are more like "Oh my God!" You may feel happy, sad, excited, angry, concerned, relieved or all of the above.

You have decisions to make, and your thoughts are whirring like a helicopter about to take off. And then it hits you. You don't ever want to work for anyone else again! You can take your skills, experience and knowledge and go to work for yourself. Haven't you been telling yourself for years that you can do it? If only you had the chance!

Guess what? You now have the chance. You are free and clear. Some people aspire to self-employment; others have it thrust upon them. It has just been thrust upon you.

Congratulations! You've just bought yourself a job.

If you are reading this book, chances are you are a business owner, executive, entrepreneur or other high level professional, who has lately come to the horrifying realization that success in business is not about *doing* what you do — it's about *selling* what you do. And while you are dynamite at doing whatever you do, this whole selling thing has you stumped.

We called this book "Selling for Geniuses" for a reason. Like you, we're sick to death of being called "Dummies" or "Idiots" just because some particular task or topic happens to be outside our area of expertise. You are a genius. That's why you are in the position you're in. If what you do were so easy, everyone would be doing it. But, if you've ever met an "absent-minded professor," or any one of those brilliant, slightly crazy people in this world that we affectionately describe as "so smart, it's amazing they can tie their own shoes," you know that genius in one arena does not always guarantee success in others. Luckily, one of the marks of true genius is to understand when to ask for help. And help is on the way!

This book is a collaborative effort among friends who also happen to be colleagues. We have all achieved a level of success in our own businesses and have faced the same struggle that you have. We've all been where you are — adjusting to a new business paradigm, looking for customers, trying to figure out how to balance our time between serving our current customers and finding new ones. We have compiled our best advice on succeeding—in sales and in business.

Let's talk about the most important subject: you. Maybe one or more of these scenarios sound familiar to you:

- You moved to a new area to start your business, and you don't know anybody.
- You retired from your company and now are consulting back to them. Your old company is your only client and you need to expand your business. How do you find more opportunities? Worse, what if you don't?
- You got so fed up with the politics at your old employer that you figured you could do it much better on your own. Now you are

discovering that running a business is really different from what you expected.

- When you opened your business and hung your shingle, you figured the business would start pouring in. You have a great reputation and a lot of contacts. You start talking to yourself, and worse, start answering yourself. What are you doing wrong?
- Once you finally get a meeting with somebody, you get into the room and you're a train wreck. Suddenly you feel like you're the new kid trying to impress the boss. You are so afraid of coming across like a used car salesman your confidence takes a nosedive.
- You have a great business, but it isn't growing the way you want it to. You have always been able to rely on word of mouth and referrals, and lately your contacts aren't delivering what you need.
- Your organization looks to you for revenue and business development leadership and you aren't sure what you need to do.

If you recognize yourself in the preceding scenarios, then this book is for you.

As an executive-level professional, you will want to approach the sales process differently from the way someone would if they were selling cookware or candy bars. You will need to seek out the right kinds of clients and develop relationships with them that benefit both of you. This book will help you do all of that, while staying focused on your goals and staying true to who you are.

We all wish you the best of success. We know you are already a genius in your main area of expertise. Using the techniques and embracing the concepts in this book will help you become a genius at selling. If any of us can help you along the way, you can find our contact information in our bios at the end of each chapter.

Get on out there, have some fun, and make some money!

—Tracy Lunquist and Chip Scholz, April, 2009

"*Don't wait. The time will never be just right.*"
—Napoleon Hill

CHAPTER ONE

Sales is Not a Four-Letter Word: "You" in a Sales Role

Susan Nielsen, President, *Leaderscapes Incorporated*

"Success is just outside your comfort zone. You've got to get uncomfortable to win." —Dr. David Yearling, Skyline Chiropractic, Burnsville, MN

What principle of selling has helped you be consistently successful?

There are four, and they are closely related:

- Choose a positive mindset
- Be authentic
- Embrace change
- Stay uncomfortable

How do you choose a positive mindset, especially about selling?

When you were a kid and people asked what you wanted to be when you grew up, you probably had something in mind like a police officer, fireman, teacher, athlete or movie star. How often does a kid respond to that question with "salesperson"? Yet, here you are, in a sales role.

For many facing the role of salesperson for the first time, the thought of having to sell can be extremely uncomfortable and fraught with negativity. Take a moment and think about the word "sales". Now think of the experiences you have had with sales people. Close your eyes and give it a good 30 seconds. Write down 8-10 words that come to mind. You have my permission to write them here in the margin.

When I do this exercise with clients, they often come up with words like "slimy, pushy, forceful, tricky, cocky and fast-talking." Sometimes they'll picture someone like Herb Tarlek from the 1970s sitcom *WKRP in Cincinnati*, in his white belt and matching shoes. He was slick, dorky, clueless, and unfortunately a very common stereotype of a salesperson. My mental image is a timeshare salesman my husband and I encountered in Florida. He was sweaty, pushy, and sexist, as well as generally hygiene-challenged. Not a great image to have.

If all salespeople fit that negative description, none of us would buy anything from a salesperson – yet, we do buy. We own cars, clothes, houses and even timeshares. So let's try the exercise again. This time, think specifically about a time when you interacted with a salesperson that was a pleasure to work with. Close your eyes again and get this person in your mind's eye. What qualities did he or she have that made him or her a great salesperson? Write down 8-10 words to describe this person and your experience.

Now, go back and read through both lists. Are they different? Of course they are. When I do this exercise with clients, their second list commonly includes words like "savvy, thoughtful, helpful, friendly, passionate, caring and pleasant" – quite a contrast to the words on the first list!

I suspect that since you are reading this book you have a desire to develop more of the characteristics in the second list. Don't the words on the second list describe who you really are?

This simple five letter word, "sales," has the power to strike fear into us at the mere thought of it, yet we all possess some of the characteristics that we find positive in other sales people. So how do you get beyond the fear and get the job done? Be more of who you really are. Be authentic.

What does it mean to "be authentic" and how will it help me sell?

It is generally accepted that people buy from people they like; I believe it goes beyond likability. People prefer to buy things they want or perceive they need from people they *trust*. People are all unique and interesting, and if you work at it, you can always find something likable, or perhaps something you can appreciate about everyone you meet. Whether or not you feel you can trust them, or that what they have will meet your needs, is another story.

Depending on the nature of your product or service sales cycle, you may have one or several opportunities with a prospect to develop a trusting relationship over time. The first impression you make is of critical importance. Each of us telegraphs the nature of our character in both visible and invisible ways, and we are more transparent than we think.

Character is made up of an individual's moral qualities, ethical standards and principles. It includes our ability to follow up on commitments, as well as our ability to laugh at ourselves and embrace our most human qualities. It is made up of our habits of thinking. Character reflects your thoughts about who you are and how you perceive the world around you. If your habits of thinking about yourself in a sales role are dominated by the negative attributes you listed in the first exercise, your prospect will sense your discomfort and negativity before a word is spoken. This will derail your sales efforts before you even start.

To get around this, people new to sales often try to "act" like they think a sales person should. They attempt to figure out what their prospect wants to see or hear and behave accordingly. More often than not, the mismatch of true belief and assumed behavior creates dissonance in the mind of the prospect. Your prospect then has to work at figuring out what is real and what is not. Is that the kind of situation you want to create?

Meet Angela. Angela is a marketing professional with a great resume and a solid track record of results. When I met her, she was being laid off and needed to find new employment. Angela was a delightful, well-spoken, confident young woman. She came to me for help preparing for an interview — the ultimate sales meeting. Despite her excellent credentials, she had not done well in interviews.

As we worked through the mock interview, Angela became increasingly uncomfortable and frustrated with herself. This driven, talented woman simply fell apart during our practice interview. Each time she stumbled, she put herself down and said something about being terrible at interviewing. She was trying so hard to be the person she thought I, as the interviewer, wanted her to be that there were no signs of the authentic, talented Angela during the interview. Unfortunately, each failed interview attempt further solidified her belief that she was terrible at interviews.

Angela did lack some interviewing skills, but that was easily corrected with some simple training. The bigger issue was getting her to quit pretending. When she focused on her negative interview experiences and tried to play a role, she acted in ways that were not representative of who she really was. Because she was incongruent, she failed to get beyond the first interview.

Similarly, if you carry negative habits of thinking about sales you will doubt yourself. When you doubt yourself, you doubt your ability or your product's ability to meet the needs of your client. If you "act" a part, your outward behaviors will expose your internal beliefs to prospective clients, expose incongruence, and create doubt in their minds. Doubt is the opposite of what you are trying to create — belief and trust.

I have confidence in my products and services, but how can I overcome negative habits of thinking about myself?

Consider who you are right now and make an "I am" list. Imagine you are peering through a window at yourself, looking from the outside in. What do you see? What strengths do you bring to your clients? What skills do you have? In what ways do you stand out? Your list might contain statements like, "I am loyal, I am friendly, I am knowledgeable about my products, I am approachable." See if you can come up with at least fifty statements. That's right, fifty.

Now look over your list. Place a check mark next to the statements that relate to success at sales. When my clients do this exercise, they typically find that all or nearly all the statements relate, and they start to see what they already bring to the table that contributes to their success.

Remember Angela? She needed to combine her strengths with some new skills in order to sell herself and win a new position. She needed to think differently about interviews and focus on her strengths. Similarly, you can combine your strengths with your sales ability and other needed skills. When you do, you are authentic. Be who you are and your results will improve.

It sounds simple, doesn't it? It's when something sounds simple that we often fail to accomplish it, because we underestimate the amount of personal change, focus, and commitment required.

So how much personal change, focus, and commitment *is* required?

Change has become a buzzword in Corporate America and around the world. It has almost as much of a negative connotation as the word sales. But all success starts with change. To make something better, you have to look at the present situation, decide to make a change, then improve and grow. Success comes as a result of improvement and growth, but the process starts with change.

In the case of improving your sales results, you must first accept that your present situation is not cutting it — you need to change in order to improve. Embracing change goes beyond the "decision" to change. You must experience a change in yourself – a shift in your thinking, in your wants, and in your willingness to be uncomfortable as you learn something new.

One of the most difficult components of real change is giving up our excuses. Our outward excuses reflect our internal habits of thinking. Our thoughts affect our behaviors; we defend our behaviors with our excuses.

What do you mean by that?

Let me give you an example. John is a retail store owner. When he opened his store about a year ago, he never imagined he would need outside sales skills. He thought that as soon as his doors were open and he and his employees provided superior customer service the business would roll in. People would come in droves, checkbooks open and credit cards out.

As you might expect, that wasn't the case. To increase sales, he would have to go out and sell. As John and I explored the world of sales and focused on building his sales skills, he made excuse after excuse for why he couldn't be successful at sales. His excuses were pretty typical. Perhaps you have heard or used some of these:

"I don't have the bubbly personality you need to be good at networking."
"I don't know what questions to ask people so I just don't talk to them."
"I feel bad about interrupting people at work so I can't do cold calls."

We all have our favorite excuses: I'm too busy, I'm too tired, I'm too stressed, I'm too cool, no one is buying, or I'm not a good sales person. Let me ask you this: when you argue for your excuses, *what do you get when you win?*

The answer is simple: when you win the argument for your excuse, you get to stay in your comfort zone, with your old habits of thinking and behaving, comfortably uncomfortable, getting the same results, recreating your "present" situation.

What are your excuses when it comes to sales? Do you recognize them when they are coming out of your mouth or going through your mind? If you truly want to change, are you ready — really ready — to let them go?

Suppose I am ready to let go of my excuses. How do I start?

Here's a great exercise. My clients have a love/hate relationship with this one. They love it because it works and they hate it because it exposes their truths. Take a sheet of paper and make three columns. At the top of the first column, write, "My excuses." At the top of the second column, write, "What I get when I win." At the top of the third column, write, "What I lose."

Now, think about your excuses. If you need to, you can borrow some of John's from the example above to get you started. Write your excuses in the first column. Then for each excuse, write down what you get — how you benefit from your excuse, and what you lose when your excuse wins. Be brutally honest. All excuses give some degree of internal satisfaction. Usually, though, the satisfaction gained is temporary while the losses are more permanent.

Remember Angela and her struggles with interviewing? Angela's excuse was that she isn't a natural interviewer. The excuse gives her the benefit of a "layer" between herself and rejection. In Angela's mind, the interviewer isn't rejecting Angela. The excuse allows her to believe that it is the "bad interview" that is being rejected. The excuse keeps Angela's perception of herself intact. What she loses is the chance at the new job.

Every time John defends his position, saying he doesn't have the personality for networking, he talks himself out of going to events and avoids being uncomfortable. He gains comfort, but loses opportunities.

Change requires you to step outside the box of your comfort zone, take risks, try new things, and be in discomfort. Unfortunately, when you are uncomfortable, your excuses have even more appeal because they help you get comfortable quickly. And, as if that wasn't enough, you have other forces working against you as well.

There will be people in your life — friends, family, colleagues and others — who will try to hold you back from attaining greater levels of success. It is not malicious; they may not even be doing it consciously. They have a picture of you in their mind. It is their habitual way of thinking about you. When you behave in ways that are consistent with their expectations they feel comfortable. When you change how you behave, however, it feels disruptive and uncomfortable for them. In their efforts to regain their own comfort, they sabotage your efforts.

When that happens, their actions may lead you to sabotage yourself. Since you are already out of your comfort zone, sliding back into your regular routine and eliminating your own discomfort is quite appealing. Soon, before you know it, you are right back where you started.

True change is hard, and it's hard from many perspectives. You've got to want it bad, and you've got to be willing to do some work to get it. Remember the quote from the beginning of the chapter: "Success is just outside of your comfort zone. You've got to get uncomfortable to win." Once you get uncomfortable, you have to find ways to stay there.

How do I go about "staying uncomfortable"?

You have likely heard the saying that there is more than one solution to every problem. There are many things you can do to stay committed to your own success. Consider doing more than one or all of them to decrease your odds of satisfying your excuses or fulfilling the wishes of others by reverting back to what is comfortable.

Find your "WHY". It is critical that you have more than just the "wish" to change. You must also have a strong desire; no, more than that: conviction. You must have a big "why". When the "why" is big enough, the "how" will happen.

I was at a training seminar about three years ago. The facilitator asked us to set a sales goal for the next quarter. I wrote down my goal on my sheet of paper, like a dutiful student. He asked me to share my goal, and then asked, "why is getting this goal important to you?" I responded with something like, "so I can achieve my sales goal for the year." He asked, "why is that important?" I said, "so I can be successful." He asked, "why is it important that you are successful?" I gave him a few more lame answers and he just kept probing further.

Then it hit me. I looked up at him with a lump in my throat, unable to speak, full of anxiety, and visibly shaken. My "why" was running through me like a river through a canyon. He smiled with a sense of knowing and looked me square in the eyes and said, "That's it. That's your why." It was my absolute, pit of the stomach, overwhelming, too raw to say out loud, "why", and the truth of it was palpable.

It is likely that you know someone who has known his or her "why." This person has gone out and achieved a goal with persistence and consistent effort, moving forward with or without help or support. I bet that if you look back over your life, you can find a time when you had that same kind of conviction – when nothing and no-one could stand in your way for long.

Your "why" can have tremendous power and influence on your behavior choices if you recognize and utilize it. You will not change if you perceive that your anxiety during and after the change will be greater than it is right now. If the idea of making the change itself is not enough to generate anxiety, we can also count on the people around us to add to it. Your "why" will help you fight anxiety's grip, motivating you to stay the course or to get back on track.

Use Your Strengths. Remember your "I Am" statements from a few pages ago? Compare your "I Am" statements to your list of excuses. Do your excuses contradict your strengths? Often they do. In order for the excuse to be true, you have to be wrong about your strength. Which is more likely to be right, your strength or your excuse? The answer depends on which you choose to make right.

You can use your strengths to help you win the fight against your excuses. Your strengths can also come in handy when those old negative thoughts about sales intrude. When you hear yourself making an excuse, out loud or in your head, fight it off by remembering your strengths.

If there is a particular excuse that gets your attention more frequently than others, consider writing an affirmation about the strengths that you have that contradict that excuse. For example, if your excuse is that you have difficulty meeting new people, but you list "friendly, generous and positive" as strengths, an affirmation like "I am a friendly, generous and positive person and people enjoy knowing me" is helpful.

Affirmations should always be written positively and in the present tense. Keep your affirmations visible and handy – posted on your wall in your office, on your computer as a screen saver, even on a card in your pocket or wallet. You never know when an excuse or other comfortable distraction will come into play.

Accept Temporary Setbacks. Success is right next to failure. The best sales people have high failure rates. They have high failure rates because they are out there doing the work, taking chances and risks, knowing that the next big success is just around the corner. They behave as if they have no fear. Everyone has fear, but successful people also have courage and faith. Courage is accepting fear as part of your life. Faith is not letting fear rule your life.

The doers in this world are the believers. They believe in their goals. They concentrate on their aim long enough to attain it. Most failure is just temporary defeat, not permanent failure. Recognize temporary setbacks, do what you must to recover, then stage a comeback and get back on track.

Acquire New Knowledge and Skills. You are in new territory. Arm yourself with the knowledge and skills you need. Become a student of those who have done what you want to do. Incorporate your learning into your goals and activities. Not up on the sales process? Having a difficult time asking for the sale or closing the deal? If there is an obstacle in your way that requires new knowledge or skills to overcome, get to class, read the book – whatever it takes to get what you need. Make continuous self-improvement and learning a priority.

Cheat! Get Help. From an early age, we are taught – and then we demand – to do things ourselves. I need look only as far as my 3-year old niece to understand how we learn to resist asking for help. I too have cheered for her when she has proudly stated "I did it by myself!"

Being the best at something is rarely a purely individual effort. Professional athletes often have multiple, specialized coaches. Actors receiving awards thank their co-stars, directors and agents for helping them bring out their best performance. Your local gym offers orientation and personal training services to help you get the most out of your workouts. My personal trainer has a personal trainer, and my coach has a coach.

A coach can help you stay focused, prepare for challenges, practice new skills, develop courage, keep the faith, push through fear, recover from setbacks, celebrate wins, challenge your self-imposed limitations, reach higher, attempt more and stay motivated. You can trust your coach not to be a dream stealer. They are there to help, guide and support you and the achievement of your goals.

Control Your Environment. You don't have control over everything, but you do have control over your immediate environment. Your environment influences your habits. Everything you see, hear, smell, touch and experience influences your thoughts, and therefore, your behaviors. For this reason, it's important to control your environment as much as possible.

What do you see and hear every day? Pay attention and make conscious choices. For example, it can be helpful to stay up on current events, but if you struggle to remain positive, the "news" can take the wind right out of your sales. Determine the best way for you to get the information you want and need without sabotaging your goals.

Seek the company of other successful people. Spend time with people who are like-minded, or possibly even those who already have the kind of success that you want. These may or may not be people you already know; you may need to go find these people and establish relationships with them. People with positive mental attitudes will inspire you with confidence. People with greater levels of success will motivate you to take risks and achieve more.

Do What Others Won't. Successful sales people do what others won't – things that other people think are too hard, too embarrassing, or too far outside their comfort zone. They lower their expectations of the people around them and raise the expectations of themselves. They commit to their goals and relentlessly work to achieve them, embracing change, accepting setbacks, and doing things that are new and uncomfortable.

Any final thoughts?

When you get past the familiar stereotypes and negative habits of thinking about sales, you'll quickly find that sales isn't a four letter word after all. You just need to re-think 'you' in a sales role. You already have much of what you need to be successful in sales; you have a unique combination of:

Strengths
Awareness of your habits of thinking, the capacity to
Learn, the ability to
Embrace change, and a commitment to your own
Success

Pepper in some focus, courage, belief, conviction, coaching and acceptance of discomfort, and you will be well on your way.

Susan Nielsen, President of Leaderscapes, partners with organizations to help them behave their way to excellence. Using individual coaching and group facilitation, Susan helps her clients bridge the gap between current and desired personal and professional success.

Susan brings 10+ years' experience in organizational and leadership development, human relations, recruiting, training and change management gained as an internal consultant and human resources professional, with specific experience leading and supporting process improvement (cycle time and variation reduction) initiatives. She has work experience in manufacturing, retail and professional services industries.

Susan holds a Master's degree in Training and Human Resource Development from the University of Wisconsin – Stout in Menomonie, WI and Bachelor's degrees in English and Mathematics from the University of Wisconsin – River Falls in River Falls, WI. She is a Qualified Administrator of the Myers-Briggs Type Indicator Instrument, a certified professional with the Total Quality Institute and an active affiliate of Resource Associates Corporation in Reading, PA. Susan received her coach training through the Resource Associates Coaching Academy (RACA) and the Coaches Training Institute (CTI) and is a graduate of CTI's Leadership program.

Susan Nielsen

Leaderscapes Incorporated
346 Soo Line Road
PO Box 1349
Hudson, WI 54016
651-214-8559
www.leaderscapes.com
susan@leaderscapes.com

CHAPTER TWO

The Four Point System

Lois Greisen, President, *Eagle Associates*

"Remember this: Whoever sows sparingly will also reap sparingly, and whoever sows generously will also reap generously." — Paul the Apostle

What principle of selling has helped you be consistently successful?

Keeping the sales funnel full is crucial. It is important to strike a balance between serving your current customers and seeking new ones. This means maintaining a consistent level of the right kinds of business activities. You can be a brilliant service professional and give outstanding service to a happy client, but you will not be successful in the long term if that happy client is your only one. It's critical to maintain a consistent level of sales activity to keep your sales funnel full.

The Four Point system described in this chapter is a structured and measurable way to develop the attitudes, behaviors, consistency and focus that drive positive sales results. It is a way to keep your funnel full. Best of all, the more you use this system, the more you can challenge yourself and reap even greater rewards.

What is a sales funnel?

Imagine a funnel shape with a wide top or entrance tapering into a narrow exit. You add prospects to the wide entrance of the funnel and move them through to the point that a sale is made as they exit through the narrow end.

You may have heard the words "suspect" and "prospect" used interchangeably. There is a difference. For purposes of this discussion, let's take a moment to define the term "prospect" in sales terms. A prospect is only a prospect if:

- They are in your target market
- They have a need
- They have the ability to pay
- They have the ability to make a decision, and
- They have scheduled a confirmed meeting with you to discuss doing business

If those conditions don't exist, they are only a "suspect" — someone who may or may not be in a position to do business with you. As you move prospects through the funnel, you make progress from the entrance to the exit of the funnel. Progress is only progress if you have a next step scheduled on *their* calendar.

If the next step is only scheduled on *your* calendar, you are really stalled until they have agreed to meet for the next step. You may have to send a letter, order a sample for them, provide some other information, do some research or something to that effect, but as long as it is only *your* action, you are stalled.

As you move your prospect down the tapered funnel toward the exit, you are aligning yourself to do business with them. An easy way to remember the steps of moving through the process of converting suspect to prospect to client is to use the acronym **SPARK.**

Suspects–	You bring in suspects from outside the funnel.
Prospects–	Once you bring suspects into the funnel, qualify them according to the definition given earlier; they become prospects. You are developing a relationship with them.
Aligning–	You are discovering their needs and aligning your product or service with those needs.
Resources–	The client is allocating their resources in the form of dollars or budgeting to purchase your product or service.
Knowledge–	You know the business is yours. That knowledge will put a SPARK into your business!

It is important to keep prospects moving through the funnel or your efforts will become stalled. Next steps must be scheduled on the prospect's calendar, not just yours. The prospect leaves the base of the funnel when the sale is made and the product or service is delivered.

What is the basis for the Four Point system?

The Four Point system is a means of tracking your sales progress to consistently move your business forward. The basis of the system is that you earn points for specific sales activities. In order to be successful, you must get at least four points per day. Point values and activities are outlined later in this chapter. If you consistently get your four points daily, you can avoid the peaks and valleys that often occur in a business.

Peaks and valleys are the curse of every small business. The syndrome is often called the "consultant's conundrum". What it means is that you are either working or you are selling. When you are selling it is because your business is slow – you have to work hard to refill the sales funnel. As a result of your activities, you generate lots of business and get overbooked. Because you are busy serving customers, you have no time to refill the funnel. You are so focused on satisfying your customers that you forget to sell! Eventually you complete the work and end up with an empty sales funnel. The cycle begins all over again.

Using the Four Point system keeps prospects consistently moving into the sales funnel no matter how busy you are. You eliminate peaks and valleys, avoiding the "feast or famine" syndrome.

How does the Four Point system help eliminate the peaks and valleys in your business?

If you consistently fill your funnel at the same time you are providing your service, you can avoid peaks and valleys. It takes dedication to do the things necessary to fill your funnel. The benefit of the Four Point system is that you decide what you need to do consistently. You develop the tasks that earn points so that you are doing the right things. Because you commit to getting your points every day, and those points add up to new business, you are assuring your own success.

Distractions often masquerade as opportunities. By determining your activities, committing to your points and working the system every day, you stay focused on the tasks at hand and avoid distractions that cost you time and money.

You probably have a pretty good idea of what those tasks are. If you don't, you will find ideas in other chapters in this book. Start jotting down your ideas as to what those tasks might be. The list will give you a good starting point as you decide the point value for your tasks.

You will need to take consistent action on those tasks. The Four Point system can help you do that. If you have small successes day in and day out, you will be successful in reaching your sales goals.

Why does the Four Point system work?

Focused activity drives results. As long as you are earning a minimum of four points each and every day, you are constantly refilling your sales funnel. Moving prospects through your funnel avoids the peaks and valleys. The peaks are wonderful; the valleys are not. When you meet your daily point goal, you have met a challenge or goal for the day and the accomplishment is a great feeling.

It works even better when rewards are tied into achieving points. Rewards may be as simple as charting your results and giving yourself a pat on the back for a job well done. Achieving a full week of points might mean a bigger reward such as going out for dinner or buying something you've been wanting. After a full month of success, reward yourself with something even bigger.

Decide in advance what your rewards are going to be. Make it something you really want. Get your family involved. You might reward yourself and your family with a family trip or something the entire family wants. Make a list of rewards, big and small, to tie to your achievements. Make it fun and exciting!

How does the Four Point system work?

The Four Point system is relatively simple. It is as easy as setting a point value for the things you need to do every day. As an example, points may be assigned in the following manner:

Task	Point Value
Leads	1
Bookings	2
Appointments Held	3
Sale	4

Leads and referrals are the building blocks of filling the funnel. They are important as a starting point, so they have a value of one point.

Booking appointments is more important than getting leads and referrals. You can collect all the leads and referrals in the world, but if you don't do anything with them, they are worthless. When an appointment is booked, it earns two points.

Appointments kept are worth three points. Getting in front of prospects to start building relationships and determine wants and needs is more important than actually booking the appointment.

Making a **Sale** gets four points. This is why you've been doing everything else! Making a sale is when you want to shout "Woo Hoo!" Getting four points for making a sale is like putting a gold star on your chart. It is your reward for your diligent and consistent work.

Once you assign points to your tasks the key is to earn a total of four points every day. For example, you might have a sale on Monday and earn four points. Your business is moving forward! On Tuesday you book an appointment for two points and meet with a different client for three points. That means on Tuesday you earned five points. On Wednesday you meet a prospect for an appointment (three points) and ask for and get a referral (one point). You have earned four points for Wednesday. On Thursday, you attend a networking event and earn four points by generating four quality leads. Finally, on Friday, you book two appointments and achieve your four points.

By totaling at least four points a day, you continue to fill and work the sales funnel at a manageable rate while still being able to serve existing clients. It is critical that you manage your time in order to complete a minimum of four points daily. It is easy to procrastinate and let one day turn into two, then three – before you know it, a week or a month has passed. Eventually your business goes into a valley. Since you are working to avoid the peaks and valleys, it is important to be consistent.

How do I know what point value to give a task?

What should you be doing every day in your business to keep moving forward? I have discussed some examples. Here are a few more:

- Write in your blog
- Network online
- Send cards to three to four people

- Write an article for a trade journal
- Call three current customers to ask how they feel you are doing for them
- Enter three people into your data management system

Give a point value for each of the listed activities and track those points until they become a habit. If you need to increase your activity level, set five or more points daily as your goal until your results improve. Make the system work for you.

The way you assign points is up to you. You may put less weight on easier or less important tasks and assign a lower point value for those tasks. More difficult or important tasks can earn higher point values. In the initial example, a lead was given one point and a sale was given four. Here is another example:

Task	Point Value
Bookings	2
Book Given	1
Cards X 3	1
Data Mgmt X 3	1
Appt Held	3
Leads	1
Sale	4

In this example, the daily goal was increased to six points. An added task was "Book Given." It related to the activity of giving a book to prospects as a marketing tactic. In your business, it might be a press kit or a catalog. "Cards X 3" meant the action of sending three handwritten cards daily to prospects and clients. "Data Mgmt X 3" meant entering three contacts into a data management system. The first two activities are business attraction and retention activities, the third an administrative function to maximize sales efforts.

Tracking all categories all of the time may not be necessary. Experiment with the categories and change them on a regular basis. Once an activity is a habit or no longer as important as it was, change what you are tracking.

You know your business. You know what you should be doing every single day...even if you are not doing those things currently. Now is the time to take the right actions.

Who can benefit from using the Four Point system?

Anyone can benefit from the Four Point system. The Four Point system is a great way to help form new habits. Any task or behavior that is required consistently can work with the Four Point system. Don't you have tasks or behaviors that you know you should be doing but aren't?

Most sources agree that it takes between twenty-one and thirty consecutive days to form a habit. Assign a point value to the things you want to make habits and track them. If you miss a day, you have to start over.

The system works for business but also can work on the personal side. One example of personal points is the area of health and nutrition. Points could be assigned like this:

Task	Point Value
Drink 8 glasses of water	1
Walk 10,000 Steps	1
20 Minutes of Weight Lifting	1
Stick to Preplanned Menu	2

The Four Point system is about being in control of your own life. Decide where and how you will use the Four Point system to improve the results that are important to you.

Should I track my points?

Absolutely! Here are the benefits of doing so:

1. See the continuous improvement in your business.
2. Reward yourself when you achieve your goal.
3. Create challenge for greater results. Solopreneurs often miss having the competition of others. Compete with yourself to get more and more points.

There are several ways that tracking points will benefit your business. For example, you might set a monthly goal to exceed the previous monthly point totals. Tie your points to your income level and give yourself a raise by making more points. Let's look at how that works.

If you decide you want to increase your income, increase your point totals. Calculate the revenue you generate from each point you earn to get a "revenue per point". If you want more revenue, get more points. When you generate more revenue, your income increases.

Tracking points may be done very simply using a legal pad and a calculator. Setting up a simple spreadsheet to do the calculations may be easier. Here is an example of a typical spreadsheet for one week:

Wk Of_____	Point Value	Mon	Tues	Wed	Thurs	Fri	Wk Totals
Leads	1		1	0			1
Bookings	2	6	2	6	6	6	26
Appt Held	3	0	0	0	3	0	3
Sale	4					4	4
Daily Totals		6	3	6	9	10	**34**

How else might you use the system?

If you have young children, chart your results together. Set up a point system for daily chores. Chart your results at the same time they chart theirs. Your kids will help hold you accountable! To increase accountability, tie a family goal to your results. Have fun with it. Get emotionally tied to the results.

Many people have created vision boards with things they want to bring into their lives. It is a great way to tie emotions to the results. By repeatedly envisioning those things that reward you, the results become much more important. For instance, I have a three ring binder full of the things that I want for my business, my family and myself. Hmm, I wonder how many points it will take to get my houseboat?

Do my values and vision affect my results?

Your vision and core values drive your behaviors. They are very important in setting and working toward your goals. Your decisions are made more easily if you base them on your vision and values. Your vision provides the guiding force for you both personally and professionally. Your values define your beliefs, your standards, and your acceptable behavior. What are your vision and personal core values? What are the vision and core values for your business?

If you base your tasks for your Four Point system on what is important to you, then you are not conflicting with your vision or values and you will feel good about your accomplishments. If you go against your core values, the opposite occurs. Your vision can motivate you to use your Four Point system and your values can define your behaviors in using the system.

How can the Four Point system help me focus?

Merriam-Webster's Online Dictionary offers the following phrases to define "focus":

- Adjustment for distinct vision

- The area that may be seen distinctly or resolved into a clear image
- A state or condition permitting clear perception or understanding
- A center of activity, attraction, or attention
- A point of concentration
- Directed attention

To be sure, clarity, vision and directed attention are critical for business success. Business people have to stay focused. Lack of focus results in working hard on many things without getting anything done. Focus is how you concentrate on the important things – those things that you need to be doing consistently. Focusing on your goals keeps you excited as well.

The Four Point system helps keep you focused on the things you need to be doing consistently to move your business forward and achieve those goals rather than jumping from one endeavor to another. Your mind can wander. You can spend time dreaming or daydreaming and not accomplish anything.

Let's see how this works in a practical setting. Take a minute right now and think only of the alphabet. Close your eyes and, in your mind, say the alphabet without allowing another thought to come into your mind. It is not easy. Be truthful, how far did you get? It's easy to let your mind wander from the task at hand, especially when the task is simple, mundane, or tedious. Staying focused can be even more challenging when the task is something you may not be fully comfortable doing, like making sales calls, or when you have other equally important tasks on your list, like serving your current customers.

By planning your activities to achieve at least four points per day, you are directing your attention where it counts. Keep your focus on the points you want to achieve every day. Develop positive affirmations around your daily tasks. "I have four points today." Or simply affirm "Four points today." One that I use is "Book four". Booking appointments is one of my keys to success. That means that I book a minimum of two appointments every day at two points each. When I focus on that, I am so excited when the task is accomplished for the day.

How does the Four Point system help with distractions?

Distractions are "life" happening. Focus is internal, distractions are external. You are pulled in many directions by outside forces. Family, friends, coworkers, employees, telephone calls and messages, email, computer glitches, and even an empty tummy can take you away from what you should be doing.

In fact, as I write this, I just received an email from someone who wants me to follow a link to another site. At the same time, my two-year-old granddaughter is here and the leg came off her doll and of course, it needs to be fixed. I am also waiting for an email from a client that will require some prep work for our scheduled meeting tomorrow. Even the lack of needed information is a distraction because when I finally get it, I will have to rearrange my schedule and figure out how to make time to get the project completed. Later, I have family coming for Sunday dinner, so it will be a challenge. This is just the weekend!

During the week, distractions are even more disruptive. Utilizing the Four Point system can help keep the distractions as distractions rather than as priorities. You keep working in the direction that *you* have predetermined. Because achieving your points is about results rather than clock times or particular methods, you can work flexibly through and around the distractions and still get the critical tasks done.

Keep your chart in front of you. Keep repeating your affirmations. Post your goals and take time to get emotionally connected with them daily. Keep your target in focus.

How does the Four Point system help with procrastination?

Procrastination is the thief of time. I have many clients who want help overcoming their procrastination. I often need the same kind of help! I think we all struggle with it at one time or another. One of the best ways that I know of to overcome procrastination is activity of any kind. A body in motion tends to stay in motion and a body at rest tends to stay at rest – any activity will get the body in motion.

Taking small steps to create activity gets the ball rolling. I had a client once who wanted to write in a journal on a daily basis. I suggested that she write one line each night. Do you think she stopped at one line? Of course not. She usually wrote at least a page if not several pages. The little activities get you moving. The Four Point system can help with those little activities. Once you are in motion, you will naturally continue to evolve your business in a positive direction.

In what ways can you use the Four Point system to schedule effectively?

Do you have a clear set of priorities? How aligned are the tasks on your Four Point system to your priorities? How motivated are you to achieve them? Perhaps you have heard the quote, "It's not how good you are, it's how bad you want it." How bad do you want to achieve your goals and grow your business? If you have carefully selected the tasks in your Four Point system so they will steadily take you toward your goals, they will be your top priority each and every day. Here are some specific pointers on scheduling more effectively:

- Choose a regular time each day to accomplish certain tasks and schedule the time in your daily planning system. Do not schedule anything in those pre-scheduled time slots and when it's time to do the tasks, get to work.

- Take consistent action. Complete the tasks and enjoy the sense of achievement from meeting the daily challenge.
- Do it again the next day.
- Do your work in batches. For example, prepare a phone list in advance so that you can make calls without wasting time looking up phone numbers.
- Schedule appointments so that they are close to each other. Save road time and put it to better use.
- If you are attending a networking event, plan in advance what you would like to achieve. Set a goal for the number of quality contacts that you would like to make.

Does My Attitude Affect My Results?

Your attitude affects everything you do. Make up your mind that you are going to make the Four Point system work for you and that you are going to do it every day. If you decide that it is bunk and think you'll just try it, chances are, it won't work for you. Henry Ford said, "Whether you think that you can, or that you can't, you are usually right."

For most people, attitudes happen by accident. They are the result of what you think about over and over. If you have a lot of good things happen, then your attitude may be more positive. If you have a lot of bad things happen, your attitude may be more negative. Eventually you can become conditioned to the negative or positive, and carry it around with you as your attitude.

Your attitudes determine your thoughts, positive or negative. Your thoughts cause your feelings. Your feelings cause your actions. Negative thoughts and feelings will cause negative actions, while positive thoughts and feelings will cause positive actions. Your actions, in turn, cause reactions, which will be either negative or positive depending on the action. This ultimately creates your results (good or bad) or lack of results.

What tasks do you enjoy doing? What don't you enjoy doing? If something that is a "must do" isn't enjoyable, it is a result of your attitude towards that task. Your thought might be: "I'll do it later". You may think subconsciously that if you don't contact a prospect, they can't say no! As long as there is hope, you may someday do business with them. Your attitude gets in the way of being effective. What is it that you are avoiding?

I realized that my attitude was affecting my business during the winter months. I live in Minnesota and we have blizzards that cause poor road and travel conditions. I used to dread having to deal with the roads and more importantly, having to cancel appointments.

When I looked closely at what I was doing, I realized what was happening. If I had to reschedule an appointment, chances were that 1) my client would understand, and 2) my client was probably in the same predicament. Once I got past that, I was fine. The attitude must be, "I am going to make this work and I am going to make it a part of my life because I want my business to move forward."

Anything else before we wrap up?

To recap the main points of this chapter:
- Understand your priorities and use the system to support them.
- Use the Four Point system every day.
- Determine what you want to earn points for, and how many you need to earn each day to achieve your goals.
- Keep your funnel full to avoid peaks and valleys in your business.
- Schedule wisely.

I wish you success in your business. You started your business for your own personal reasons. Keep those reasons in mind at all times, especially when the going gets tough. Using the Four Point system will help you in the areas where you need it most. Make it work for you. Challenge yourself, keep stretching, and never let your sales funnel run dry.

Lois Greisen, president and owner of Eagle Associates, is an executive coach, trainer and public speaker. She is a Certified Professional in InnerMetrix's Attribute Analysis, and has been a Mastermind Member for Resource Associates Corp., based in Pennsylvania since 2002. In addition, she is a certified consultant for KeyneLink, providing a web based Strategy Execution system (Strexecution). She is a Certified Business Coach and works with CEOs and corporations across North America. Lois is also a LifeSuccess Coach working with Bob Proctor from the movie and book, *The Secret*. *LeaderScopes*, a monthly newsletter produced and written by Lois, is distributed broadly.

Lois's professional practice focuses on helping companies develop and implement their strategic plans and coaching executives and their teams to follow through execution of the plan. The outcomes include achieving organizational initiatives, performance improvement, building high performing teams and personal and professional development.

A strong supporter of the community, Lois is a member of five area chambers of commerce, Rotary Club of Perham, MN, and is currently a board member of The Minnesota Chapter of the American Society for Clinical Laboratory Science, serving as an Area Director. Lois holds a master of Science degree in Clinical Laboratory Science and has over 20 years of management experience.

Lois Greisen
Eagle Associates
Frazee, Minnesota 56544
Phone: 218-334-3744
Cell: 218-841-4179
www.eaglea.com
greisen@arvig.net

CHAPTER THREE

Selling is NOT Accidental!

Chip Scholz, Head Coach, *Scholz and Associates, Inc.*

"To be outmaneuvered? Yes. To be surprised? Never!"
—Napoleon Bonaparte

What principle of selling has helped you be consistently successful?

Relationships are the key. You will never build a long term, sustainable, successful business without building relationships. It just won't happen. A relationship is defined as a relatively long-term association of two or more individuals, brought together for a common purpose and mutual benefit.

The crucial element for successful selling is forming the right relationships. Not every relationship will move both parties in the direction they want to go. Long-term, sustainable success in sales only happens when there is mutual benefit. You have to put yourself in front of the right people at the right time with the right message so there is shared value in the relationship. Building relationships improves your odds of making the sale. That takes planning.

I remember my father using an old adage while I was growing up, and I think it is applicable here. He told me "Never marry for money. Just go where money is and fall in love." What he was talking about was creating a relationship that had mutual benefits through proper planning.

The problem is that most sales books focus solely on what to do once you are in front of the customer. That is important, but not as important as understanding the context of the sales encounter. You won't be able to do that unless and until you have set yourself up to be successful.

In my coaching practice, I use four words to help clients define and pursue what they want. Those four words are *clarity, focus, attention and intention*. They resonate in sales as well. You will read about each word and its relation to sales later in the chapter, but here is a brief discussion of each one.

Clarity Having a clear definition of the clients you want to do business with. How are you positioned in the marketplace and in the minds of your prospects? Once you have clarity about your position, you can sell more effectively.

Focus What is your level of effort in going after your clearly defined markets? How focused are you on getting business on board from your targets? Remember that distractions often masquerade as opportunities—and they can take away your focus.

Attention Are you continually scanning the environment, paying attention to opportunities that fall within the clearly defined parameters you have focused on?

Intention Are you working in an intentional manner, setting goals about your accounts and your activities and then achieving measurable results? How are you intentionally creating the relationships you have planned?

What is the first step in sales planning?

Decide to become an expert. What is it you are an expert in? If you answer only that you are an expert in your business, then you are probably starving. As a professional who sells, you must have expertise in three areas to be effective.

1. *It is important to know what your business is.* Since you are most likely the person primarily responsible for delivery of your services, you ought to be pretty good at what you do. Even if you have a company to back you up, the company needs to provide a high level of service. Your confidence in your abilities and those of your company, or lack thereof, will be amply evident to your customer. Even if you are not a complete subject matter expert you should have confidence in your ability to deliver what you intend to sell.

There is a downside to the expertise, though. When you are too reliant on your subject matter expertise, you may end up talking yourself out of a sale. Experts often have to show that they are experts, don't they? How many times have you met someone and asked what he or she does, only to have him or her throw up on your shoes? They hurl a verbal onslaught at you that makes you want to duck and find cover.

Think of this area of expertise more in terms of self-confidence. You don't have to show how smart you are to make a good impression on a prospect. Instead, make your expertise the foundation of your self-confidence.

2. *It is important to know how your prospects and clients do business.* How much or how little you need to know about your customer and their industry depends on the technical nature of your product or service. When you work in only a few market verticals, you have a chance to become well known in those verticals. You will be seen as an expert in those areas.

When I started my business I was fond of saying: "It's not important that I know what they do, but it is really important that I know what I do." I needed to say that to convince my customers and myself. The truth is that customers don't care what you do unless they know why it is important to them. It becomes important to them because you know their business. Customers want to have some level of comfort that you can speak their language.

3. Nothing else is nearly as important as being an expert in sales! I know a lot of gifted people that are experts in their business or a particular industry, but they end up starving if they can't get someone to pay for their services. I am approached frequently by people who are gifted facilitators, speakers, coaches and consultants. They want to "partner" with me, which means that they want me to be the rainmaker and toss them business. If you can't be an expert at selling, you will have great difficulty staying in business.

What other elements are important when planning your sales efforts?

There are three elements to the planning stage. The elements are: Proper Positioning, Paying Attention and Planning the Call.

What is proper positioning?

Part 1 of proper positioning is all about **CLARITY**. I recently had a conversation with a friend of mine, an attorney, who was always looking for more business. He certainly wasn't a salesperson, but knew that he had to sell to make a living. One night he stood up in our networking group and said: "A good referral for me is anyone that needs a lawyer."

I pulled him aside after the meeting and asked him if what he said was true. He replied "yes". I then said, "In other words, anyone that can fog a mirror and pay you with a check that won't bounce is a good customer for you?" He nodded. "So someone getting a divorce would be a good referral?" I continued. He said no, he didn't do divorces. I asked "What about someone that has an immigration problem?" He said no, he didn't do immigration issues.

I then asked him the $1 million question: "Well then, we know what you don't do. What is it that you do?" and with that he was able to clearly explain an ideal client for his practice. That kind of clarity is what it takes to be successful in any business.

The story about the attorney illustrates positioning. Positioning is the ranking or perception that potential clients have of you relative to your competition. How do your competitors perceive you? How are you perceived in the marketplace? Do you know how you are positioned? Do you know who your competition is?

For most professionals, competition is really difficult to gauge. If you are engaged in just about any kind of professional enterprise that can be described as a practice, there are a lot of competitors out there. In the prospective client's mind, they all doing the same things you are.

There is no difference between you and every other competitor out there...*unless* you position yourself properly. It is far better to define your position and be able to communicate it than have your competition or your prospect do it for you.

To position yourself in a way that sets you apart from the competition, clearly define what market you want to be in or the opportunities you want to take advantage of. By defining the opportunities, you are also defining the kinds of relationships you want. Markets, opportunities and relationships can be defined in a number of ways. Here are a couple of ways of defining markets. This is not a complete list but is probably a good start:

Geographic – just as described, your focus is on anyone that needs your services within a defined geographic area. This may be the primary way to define a market for businesses that rely on traffic coming to them such as a retail store or doctor's office.

Industry – it could be very broad or very narrow. Manufacturing would be a broad definition; roller bearing manufacturing would be narrow.

Function – job titles are a good way for some services to position themselves. It may be a focus on C-level executives (CEO, COO, CFO, CIO, CMO, CTO, etc.), sales, floor supervisors, etc.

Ownership or company maturity – some people like working with privately held companies, some like publicly traded companies. Early stage startups make great clients for some, others need to work with a more mature business.

Specialty – if you are a subject matter expert, then the subject matter tends to define the markets.

Once you have determined your market, learn as much about it as you can. Here are some ways to learn what you need to know to position yourself effectively:

- Research the organizations that your potential customers belong to and join them. Become active. Go to the meetings, dinners, and conferences.
- Read all of the trade journals and publications you can about your chosen market. Read what your prospects are reading.
- Search the web. See what others are saying about your potential clients. What are their unique needs, wants and issues?
- Gather as much information as you can about your competition in an ETHICAL manner.

If you work diligently, you will develop a good deal of market intelligence. Once you do, it is time to put it to use by attracting others to build a business relationship with you.

You mentioned clarity and focus. We have covered clarity. What does focus have to do with proper positioning?

FOCUS is about knowing your target and then putting yourself in the position of engaging them. Most professionals don't take the time to write a list of the companies or individuals in their target market. The list could be made up of the actual businesses and people you want to engage. The list could also be people that influence your market. When you take the time to list the names, you bring them into your focus. They are there, written down, real, in black and white – in FOCUS.

You may not be able to do business with them right away. Some of them are going to take a long time to get into, or they may not need your services right away. Some are going to require you to learn new skills, acquire new ways of doing your business, or just add more experience. If they are in your target market, they should be written down. By keeping your focus on specific companies or people, you will be able to find ways of attracting them when the time is right for you to work together.

The point is that you have to understand what your target market is, build credibility in your target market and put yourself in the position to meet and engage with your targets. That takes planning, thought and a lot of work before you ever actually make a sales call.

Clients don't do business with you when you want them to. They only do business when they want to do business with you. One of the biggest mistakes a business owner or sales person can make is to have too few opportunities to work on. You only get desperate when you have most of your eggs in one basket. When you are so intent on one or two opportunities, you tend to be really frustrated, nervous, anxious and desperate. Nothing smells worse to a potential client than the stink of desperation.

Once you have a list of target opportunities, what should you do with it?

The next step is to implement an active marketing approach. There are several ways of creating focus on your target relationships, but the point is to make them aware of you. There are a number of effective ways to do that, many discussed in this book. Here are a few that you may find helpful.

Be visible. You have joined the organizations that your potential clients are a part of. Now become involved! Not just on the periphery, but in the mainstream. Write articles for the organization's publications. Offer to speak at their conferences. Put yourself where they are...the target rich environments.

Here is a little known secret that has to do with trade organizations and their communication channels. You may think that it is difficult to get published in trade journals and other communication organs. I suppose if you want to get published in the Journal of the American Medical Association it might be. However, many organizations are starving for content. When I first got involved in my target market, I had lunch with a target market association executive and offered to write a column for him. He was encouraging but hesitant, and I couldn't understand why. When I sent him the article, he called me and made it clear why. He told me that several people had offered to write content for him, but no one had ever actually done it!

Ask your target market. If you want to be well known and be considered an expert in the industry, ask questions of the people in it. Put together four or five questions of general interest to the market segment you are targeting. Call ten or more of the people you want to get to know. Tell them that you are doing a survey and would like their input, and that you will send them the information once you have put it together. Interview them on industry trends, business conditions, things that you would like to know. Ask them about the challenges they are facing, and what they are doing about those challenges. Do not engage them in a sales conversation at this point.

Once you have done the research there are many ways to disseminate the information. Put a brief report together with your findings and offer it to the trade association for publication. Offer to give a speech, a teleconference, a briefing or any other kind of interpersonal gathering to discuss your findings. Send a professional looking report to the people that participated, asking them if you might have a moment of their time to discuss the results.

Reach out. Develop and distribute your own monthly or quarterly newsletter. You can do this in an electronic or hard copy/mailed format, or both. If you are unsure about your ability to write or be disciplined enough to put out your own content, there are several resources that can provide you content. Several even have customizable newsletter formats that are point and click solutions.

An e-mail newsletter is a great way to push content to a large number of people, but you may want to try a different approach for the most likely targets. Using a list of the top 20-40 targets (and current customers) send them "lumpy mail" on a regular basis. Lumpy mail is any kind of mail that puffs an envelope. It could be a small gift, a laminated card containing tips for their use or any kind of relevant article. It could even be a newspaper article you have seen about that company.

Make sure that you are providing value in your content and not a sales pitch. Give tips and free information that will help people feel comfortable with you. Tailor the content to the target audience you want to reach.

If you are marketing locally, dropping something off for the decision maker can work. For example, there was a prospect I really wanted to get in to see and it just wasn't happening by phone, networking or in person. So, I started dropping by once a month with a dozen donuts. I put my card on the box with a note to the decision maker, saying "Hi." I didn't make a point of asking for an appointment. I was just saying hello.

The person eventually became curious and agreed to see me. That company became one of my biggest clients.

Be easy to find. A website is a good way to be accessible. However, it is no longer enough. A website is just the price of entry to the market. Web 2.0, social networks, blogging and new media are buzzwords that add up to having others pull your content to them rather than trying to attract prospects to a static resource like your website.

Blow your own horn! No one else is going to. Hire a public relations expert if you aren't comfortable doing it yourself. You want to send a continual flow of up-to-the-minute news releases of your successes to the media outlets your targets read, view or listen to.

Show off! Offer free how-to-do-it seminars or workshops for associations that your targets do business with. Make them valuable, non-commercial and geared to your targets. If you are targeting CEOs, host the session in an upscale venue like a dining club or elegant restaurant.

A great way to accomplish this and get a better mix of potential clients is to work with strategic partners. Work with other business professionals that have non-competing products or services. Put on a seminar that creates a total solution to solve your mutual target's problems.

For instance, if you are a coach or a consultant, you may want to partner with an accountant, an attorney and labor specialist to do an executive briefing. Each person is responsible for bringing three or four executives to the briefing and for providing 15-20 minutes of content. That way you have a mix of people and ideas that makes the event even more profitable.

Be patient. None of the above steps are instant business attractors. They are designed to build relationships over time and put your business on a firm foundation for long term, sustainable success.

You mention that Paying Attention within your target market is the second step. Isn't that what most people call prospecting?

Yes, it is, but there is a distinct difference.

What is the difference to you?

You have to pay **ATTENTION**, be aware, to see the opportunities when they come around. It is kind of like watching trout in a stream going after a fresh insect hatch. Let me take you to my favorite stream.

It is spring, and the water and air are still crisp and cool. The water below you is a mixture of action and calm. Hanging over the water, you notice columns of insects in a pillar shape. On first look, they look pretty stable, but as you look closer, you see that they are actually in constant motion. They are mixing and moving, going from one level of the pillar to the other. At the bottom of the pillar you catch a flash of silver or gold as the trout jump and catch the insects that have flown closest to or landed on the river.

Not all insects are eaten. Some escape and fly back higher in the column for a while until they tire and swoop back down to the water where they are back in range for the trout. Some are blown off course and end up over land where the trout aren't able to get to them.

As you scan the river, you find that there are schools of trout under the columns. However, there are trout swimming in other areas, not paying attention. They are missing the dance of insects that is ringing the dinner bell for others. Sound familiar?

Like trout looking for the hatch, some of us are in the right place doing the right things and are getting business. There are some potential clients that fall within our grasp, ready to buy what we are selling. There are some that come close but then fly back higher, out of reach. There are some that fly away, never to be seen again.

Remember that not every potential client is going to do business with you. You are not going to be right for everyone. That's why there are so many people in your business, and so many clients out there to be served. At this point it might be appropriate to introduce you to a very important principle for sales, and for keeping your sanity. *SWSWN: Some Will, Some Won't... NEXT!*

Your job is to make sure you have enough of the right clients positioned well so that when they come close enough to engage, you are paying attention to the possibility.

How does paying attention translate to action in the real world?

The better job you do of finding and attracting qualified prospects, the more business you will do. If you are paying attention, those clients who can be attracted to you can be defined as those who:

- Have an identifiable need, are aware of that need and are paying attention to it. People may not know they have a need for your services, but they may have issues that call for your solutions.

- Have the ability to pay for your services. This means that they can actually write you a check or cause a check to be written to you. Do they have the authority to make a deal?

- Have a sense of urgency to do something. The problem or issue is so big that it is causing problems for them that are worth paying you to help solve.

- Have trust in you. If you have done your job in building your credibility, these people will listen to you and be willing to accept your solutions.

A great salesperson I had the opportunity to get to know was Bill Brooks, founder and owner of the Brooks Group. Bill passed away a few years ago, but his work lives on in his books and the business run by his sons. One of my favorite quotes from Bill about prospects was, *"In a highly competitive crowded marketplace, all other things being equal, the one with the most information about the prospect and market, who knows how to turn it into solutions, will win the sale."*

It sounds like you are describing ways of warming up the sale rather than just making a bunch of cold calls. Is that right?

Yes, and that brings me to the final part of the process. That is **INTENTION**. What are you *intentionally* going to do? Let's apply it to a specific activity – networking.

Let's assume for a moment that you have done your work and positioned yourself well. You have a great list of targets that you are actively marketing. You are sending the newsletters, lumpy mail and are doing everything right. You still aren't able to get any traction. What will help?

Intentional networking is the key, and it is based on the fact that people expect you to make claims about your products or services, they expect you to make the phone calls, but they are really impressed when others carry your message for you. There is nothing like an introduction from a trusted associate to open doors.

When I began my own coaching, speaking and writing business, we had just moved to Charlotte, North Carolina from Los Angeles. We knew exactly five people in Charlotte – two realtors, the builder and his rep and the lawyer who closed the deal on the house we built. We had moved 2500 miles from all of our contacts and opened a business dependent on contacts. It wasn't exactly the best base from which to get a business launched!

I had to build a network, and I had to build it fast. In the early stages of my business, I decided to take a geographic and subject matter focus for my business. I chose that focus because I wasn't sure how to market myself outside the local area. I had subject matter expertise in the solid waste business, transportation and local government. Those companies that were within a half-day drive and fell within those markets became my focus.

Don't think that these were the only clients that I would work with. I was open to the possibilities of working with other market verticals. However, I was paying more attention to the organizations that were within my target. I then went to work on attracting the kind of network that would allow me to build credibility in those markets. Thus, the "Five by Five" program was born.

Simply stated the "Five by Five" program is about exponentially expanding your network and building relationships with your target market. Your objective is to get five names to contact from each person you meet. The multiplier effect is amazing. Here's the practical application of the program.

The Five by Five Program, Step One:

It starts by contacting someone within your target market that is an influencer. It might be a market leader, the head of the industry association or chamber of commerce, or a community leader that has a number of contacts. Since you are not selling at this point, only building a network, it is easier to get an appointment with those people. The initial phone contact goes something like:

"Hi, my name is Chip Scholz. I am new in the community (or business sector, or market vertical – your market position), and I was wondering if I could buy you a cup of coffee and ask a few questions. I understand you know quite a bit about (the business, the community, etc.) and I would like to pick your brain. I could really use your help. Do you have time next Tuesday at 3 o'clock?"

There are four key concepts that open doors in the previous statement:

- You want their help. It is a fundamental need of human beings to want to help their fellow humans. Since you are not selling to them, they are more open to helping you.
- You are positioning yourself as someone that is there to learn, not there to tell them anything. You are not throwing up on their shoes. They are going to want to know what you do, and that is where a positioning statement is important, but their first impression should be that you want to learn.
- You have positioned them as the expert. Flattery can get you a lot of places WHEN it is sincere and directed.
- You are being specific about setting a time. If you don't, they won't. Be sure you have a suggested meeting time.

Step Two, The Meeting:

A meeting can take place over the phone or in person. If you are marketing over the phone, you might be able to have the meeting by merely asking if it is a good time to talk when making the initial call. Or you may want to set up a separate phone meeting.

Once you are in the meeting, no matter whether it is face to face or over the phone, be prepared. Have a list of questions that you want to ask ready for the meeting. Ask general, open-ended questions. Some suggested questions might be:

- Tell me a little bit about the _____ (industry, community, etc.).
- What are the major issues facing it?
- If I were to get involved, what are the best ways to get involved?

Spend 15 or 20 minutes gathering information and getting to know the contact. You are earning the right to ask the key questions of the Five by Five program. Those questions are:

"If I want to know more about (the community, the business, etc.) who are the five people I need to meet? Do you have their contact information, and would you mind if I used your name if I called them?"

I have found that most people give five names, and those that don't give five will give one, two or three names. SWSWN applies in this step – SOME WILL give you names, SOME WON'T, NEXT!

Step Three, Follow Up:

This is a vital step in building your network and one that is most often forgotten. You must follow up with the people you were introduced to. You must also follow up with the initial contact. Here are some tips for follow up:

1. Learn the power of the handwritten card. Get a note card made with your logo on it. Handwrite thank you notes to everyone you see. Not many people take the time to handwrite anymore. It will create an impression with the person receiving it because you took the time to do it. A handwritten card generally gets through the clutter of other mail. If your handwriting isn't good, then write it out in block letters or get someone else with better handwriting to write it for you.

2. Use the process for making and completing appointments with each subsequent contact.

3. Every time you have a meeting with a contact that was suggested to you, write another thank you note to your original

contact. It is a great way for them to track your progress, and will remind them why they trusted you in the first place.

4. Keep a list of the people and their connections. In a way, it is like an up close and personal LinkedIn or Facebook. You are creating the network, so track it!

The end result? A large number of relationships. Some of them will turn into customers, some won't. Some will become colleagues, some will become referral sources. However, if you faithfully apply Five by Five, you will soon run out of time to keep expanding the network. You will get to the point where you will just be too busy. Isn't that the point?

Would you mind summarizing the key points?

In this chapter, we have discussed a number of strategies that, if implemented, will substantially improve your odds of making more sales. If you want to close more business more often, more profitably, remember these four words: Clarity, Focus, Attention and Intention.

Clarity—Know the relationships you want to foster and the target markets you want to be in.

Focus—Put your efforts into a focused campaign that maintains a consistent level of activity to attract the relationships you want.

Attention—Constantly scan your environment keeping an eye out for opportunities to build your target relationships.

Intention—Intentionally build your personal network by practicing active referrals using the Five by Five program.

Good luck and good selling!

Henry E. "Chip" Scholz is Head Coach of Scholz and Associates and is an executive coach, columnist and a public speaker. He is a member of Target Training International's Chairman's Club and Resource Associates Corporation's Senior Mastermind Group. He is a Certified Business Coach and works with CEOs, elected leaders, and decision makers across North America. "The Scholz Report", Chip's monthly newsletter, is distributed broadly. His book, *Do Eagles Just Wing It?* is due to be published in 2009.

Chip's professional practice focuses on executive coaching, assessments for selection and hiring, speaking and writing. As a public speaker, he has presented to businesses, civic groups and professional associations throughout the U.S. and Canada.

A strong supporter of the community, he has served as Chairman of the Board of four chambers of commerce. Chip has founded four community organizations, including the South Bay Police and Fire Memorial Foundation in the South Bay area of Los Angeles County, which has raised more than $1 million for police and fire personnel since 1994. In addition, he has held advisory positions in state, county and local government, including chair of the Los Angeles County Quality and Productivity Commission.

Chip currently serves on the board of the International Warehouse Logistics Association in Chicago.

Chip Scholz
Scholz and Associates, Inc
PO Box 611
Cornelius, NC 28031
Office: 704-827-4474
Cell: 704-400-6926
www.Scholzandassociates.com
chip@scholzandassociates.com

CHAPTER FOUR

Transformational Networking: Getting More Business in the Best Possible Way

David Emery Smith, President, *Performance Dynamics Systems*

"You can have everything in life that you want if you will just help enough other people get what they want." —Zig Ziglar

What principle of selling has helped you to be consistently successful?

Building a network of quality contacts and creating relationships is critical to success in sales. I call this process "transformational networking." Transformational networking requires three things: people must know you, like you, and trust you. There are specific principles you can apply to build "know, like and trust" with the people you meet. The application of these principles will transform your networking behaviors and enhance the quality of your relationships.

In our highly interconnected world, interpersonal relationships are more important than ever. The world is filled with opportunities for you to provide value to others through the goods and services you offer. The chance of being in the right place at the right time to satisfy that need is small. If you have a large and effective business network, your likelihood of getting in front of people at their moment of need increases exponentially. Your network expands and extends your sales efforts.

Networking is an effective way of growing a business because people want to do business with others they know. The perception is that buying from someone we know, even casually, is a much lower risk than buying from a stranger.

As a person engaged in the selling process, you will be much more comfortable going into a potential sales opportunity when the prospective client has been "warmed up" by a referral from someone who knows, likes and trusts you. There's just much less anxiety all the way around when dealing with someone with whom you have a connection. Therein lies the value of referrals. A referral gives you instant credibility, borrowed from the person who has provided the referral.

This "halo effect" of borrowed credibility cuts both ways. If you get a referral into an opportunity and fail to treat the prospective client with courtesy and professionalism, it is a negative reflection on you and the person who provided the referral. Therefore, you are honor-bound to treat a referral in the most professional manner possible.

Is networking a good way to get customers?

It is the BEST way to get customers, but not necessarily in the way you think. When you meet people through networking, don't view them only as potential customers. View them as people who might know your potential customers. Explain what you do, what kinds of problems you solve, and what kinds of benefits people get from working with you. If you think of your new acquaintance as a point of connection rather than as a potential customer, it takes pressure off both of you.

Think about it this way: if there is a five percent chance any one person might see the benefit from your product at any one point in time, talking to someone about your product yields a five percent chance that you can productively begin the sales process with that person, and you have to talk to (on average) twenty people for one sales opportunity.

On the other hand, if the average person knows twenty people, everyone you talk to can give you one qualified referral. The irony is that approaching a person as a potential referral source rather than as a potential customer makes it more likely that they will be both, because that approach generally circumvents their defensive barriers. Don't use this as a manipulative ploy, however. People will sense it and you will get neither orders nor referrals. Remember, the key is to generate *know, like,* and *trust.*

The title of your chapter is Transformational Networking. How is networking transformational?

Networking is not inherently transformational. Networking can be done well, or done poorly. Becoming a more effective networker requires you to transform your attitudes and behaviors. In turn, identifying and adopting new attitudes and behaviors transforms *you* into a more effective networker. Being a more effective networker is the first step in getting the results you want—more revenue and more profitable customers.

The essence of transformational networking is summarized in the motto of one of my mentors, Frank Agin: "become the person you want to network with." Let's talk about how that works. Here is an example of someone who absolutely did not understand the attitudes and behaviors required to be successful in networking.

- He never wanted to get to the referral group meeting a minute early. Most of the time he arrived just in time. Many times he was late.

- Because he did not arrive early, he never got a chance to socialize with the group before the meeting, and missed that opportunity to build relationships with the other members.
- Most people stayed around to socialize for a while after the meeting was over. Not this guy. As soon as the meeting was over, he took off like his car was about to get towed.
- His chapter scheduled a social event once a month so people could get to know each other better. He never attended these events. He always said he was too busy, even though he really wasn't.
- He avoided taking on a leadership position. He made excuses. He would say he didn't have enough experience. He said he needed a better understanding of the responsibilities of the officers. In reality, he was not interested in doing the work and did not see the value of the opportunity.
- When he finally did take a leadership position, he did the minimum and never really engaged with his duties.
- He contributed the bare minimum of referrals. He saw the referral group as a 75 minute a week commitment. He usually thought of referrals during the meeting so he could meet the letter of his chapter's expectations, and because of that his referrals were of low quality.

This guy just didn't get it. He failed to make a genuine commitment to his chapter and to networking in general. He gave a minimal effort, and he got minimal results.

Confession: I was that guy!

That referral group fell apart, so I joined another one. I did a little better, but my participation was not where it needed to be. I was eventually asked to leave the chapter.

I may be slow, but I'm not stupid. I had learned networking was a great way to build my business, so I started my own referral group. I finally paid attention to the lessons of the previous two attempts. The lights started to come on. I finally began to understand what successful networking is all about. Just like all pursuits, your results are proportional to the effort you make. When I finally understood what I needed to do, the group worked. My results reflected my efforts.

How do I become the person I would want to network with?

Give first. You have to give to get. The best way to get referrals is to provide something of value. If you want a referral from someone, provide a referral for him or her first. If you are not in a position to provide a referral offer a small favor: an introduction to another person; an article on a subject of interest; or anything the other person may value. You don't have to give away goods and services for free, but you have to provide value people recognize.

How do I generate know, like, and trust?

These three states are sequential. One builds on another. People generally won't trust you unless they like you. They can't like you unless they know you. The way for people to know you is for you to get out there and mingle. Follow the three-foot rule. When you are in a social setting, talk to somebody whenever they get within three feet of you.

What do I say?

It's pretty straightforward. Introduce yourself, ask the other person their name, and ask them what they do.

Are people going to want to talk to me because they want to help me?

Some will, but most will want to talk to you because **you** want to help **them**. Remember, the first step in transformational networking is "give to get". You will feel a lot less self-conscious about talking to people when you know your objective is to help them and provide referrals to them. They will feel a lot less stressed when they know it too.

How can I be likeable?

First impressions are very important in networking situations. Remember, be the person you would want network with. The root of this is to be the person you would want to engage in conversation. Here are a few tips for being approachable:

1. Personal appearance is important. Take reasonable care in your appearance without being preoccupied with yourself. Dress for success — most people act more professional when they wear a suit, even if they don't realize it.
2. Smile! When you smile, you are much more approachable and appear to be friendly.
3. Take a sincere interest in the person you want to network with. You can show interest by asking non-threatening questions that allow for open conversation.
4. Allow the other person to speak, if they want to. Studies have shown that when you listen attentively to another person, they will remember you as being more interesting!
5. Be focused on them, not on you.
6. Look for ways that you can help them by asking how you might be of help to them. Giving a referral is the best way to do so.

How do I generate trust?

Trust has two time frames: short term and long term. Generating short-term trust is a function of a good first impression followed by developing rapport. The way in which you communicate should depend on the behavioral style of the other person. When you recognize, understand and appreciate the behavioral styles of others it builds rapport quickly.

Adapting to behavioral styles works on the premise that we are more willing to trust people that are like us. Until you can understand the behavioral style, begin all interactions in neutral. When you approach others in neutral there is time to understand, recognize and appreciate, then adapt. When you do it right, it builds trust.

While there are many combinations of styles, there are four general categories of behaviors. Here is a quick overview of the styles and how you might adapt to them:

Behavioral Characteristics	How To Adapt
When communicating with a person who is ambitious, forceful, decisive, strong-willed and goal-oriented	• Be clear, brief, and to the point • Stick to business • Be well organized

When communicating with a person who is magnetic, enthusiastic, friendly, demonstrative, and political	• Provide a warm and friendly environment • Ask "feeling" questions to draw their opinions, especially about people • Let them guide the conversation
When communicating with a person who is patient, predictable, reliable, steady, relaxed and modest	• Begin with a personal comment to break the ice • Take your time and present your opinions in a non-threatening way • Ask "how?" questions to draw their opinions
When communicating with a person who is dependent, neat, conservative, perfectionist, careful and compliant	• Be prepared, professional, and organized • Stick to business • Use facts and accurate details to support your arguments

© Target Training International, LTD.

Most people are a blend of two or more of these behavioral patterns. Be sensitive to which pattern is most pronounced in a person at a given moment, and be alert to when there is a shift in which pattern is dominant.

The best way to generate long-term trust is to honor your commitments. When you give your word, keep it! Follow up when you say you will. Call when you say you will. Do the work that you say you will.

The words that should guide you in generating trust, and in transformational networking in general, are: "become the person you want to network with." Hold yourself to that standard. Reflect on your past actions, assessing them against that standard. Plan your future actions against that standard. Your pursuit of that standard will guide your transformation.

What's your definition of a referral?

A referral may be described in several ways. For our purposes, the best functional definition is "a person or business that has a reasonable need for your goods and services." In addition, there is an expectation that when a call is made to them, it will be answered favorably.

A referral differs from a lead in a very basic way. A lead is when you tell someone the name and number of a possible suspect even though there is no relationship and no expectation of action.

For instance, a lead for a real estate broker might be the address of a "For Sale By Owner" house. It's better than going through the phone book, but only a little better. If you know the homeowner, give the owner the business card of the broker, and you have determined that the owner is willing to take a call from the agent, then it becomes a referral.

A referral is actionable and carries value to the person who receives it. A lead is nice, but carries little value. Referrals build trust and commitment. Leads do not. To build trust, be the person who gives high quality referrals.

Who is the best person to ask for a referral?

You can ask anyone for a referral. Your satisfied customers are the most likely source for great referrals for you. Other sources are friends, complete strangers, acquaintances, and family members. Wherever you have the opportunity to network, you can get referrals.

How do I ask a customer for a referral so that they give me one?

Success in getting referrals from a customer is largely a function of how, and when, you ask for the referral. It takes preparation. From the beginning of your relationship with your client, establish the expectation that when they experience value from working with you, you will be asking for a referral. Build it in up front. It plants the seed and gives the customer time to get used to the idea.

When you ask for a referral, **don't** say something like "I build my business through referrals. Do you know anybody who would be willing to talk with me?" Instead, be alert for those occasions when your customer acknowledges value from your work together. When the customer acknowledges value, thank them and then say something like, "I am glad you have received value from our work together. Who else do you know that might benefit from working with me?" What you say, and when you say it is important.

I've gone to some networking meetings but I haven't gotten much out of them. It doesn't seem like it's worth the time and effort.

Remember the story about the guy who went through three networking groups before he figured out the value? It's not always easy to fully embrace networking. It takes commitment and willingness on your part to change your attitudes. The hardest part is getting started.

For example, the local business journal in Columbus, Ohio sponsors a great networking breakfast every other month. It starts at 7:00 AM. Every time it rolls around I struggle to get up. I have a dialog in my head, as I am sure you do in similar circumstances. One part of me tries to convince the rest of me that it's okay to skip the event just this one time and sleep in. It takes some willpower to get out of bed, take a shower, put on a suit and tie, and hit the road before dawn. I do it because my business will suffer if I don't, and I am always glad afterward that I went.

If you need some extra help, get a commitment partner. A commitment partner is another professional who is also going to the networking meeting. By holding each other accountable, and creating peer pressure, you each will have more reason to go.

Commitment partners are useful in another way. Have you ever walked into a crowded room where everyone seems to be in the middle of an intense conversation? Do you sometimes feel like an outsider? Do you just want to turn around and leave? Don't do it. Rely on your commitment partner.

Even if you don't have a partner, there is a solution. Look around the room for another person who looks like they feel like you do. Walk up to them, introduce yourself, and find out how you can help them. Then pair up and work the networking event together.

Your attitude walking into a crowded room should be: "What a target rich environment! How many people in this room can I help today?" I have put together a white paper to help you get the most out of a networking meeting. You can get it at www.pdsystems.net/NetworkMeetings101.

What's the difference between a networking meeting and a referral group?

A networking meeting is a random collection of people. Many of the people found in a networking meeting are strangers. You probably have never met them before and, unless the event is sponsored by a membership organization like a chamber of commerce, you will rarely see them again. It is random, so your results are random. Even in the case of repeating events that attract many of the same people again and again, the people at the event tend to focus on selling to each other, not on building referral relationships.

A referral group is different from a networking meeting. Membership in a referral group is usually restricted to one person in each business category. The other members of a referral group act as an extension of your sales efforts. Members support each other by selling *through* each other rather than *to* each other. Giving and receiving referrals is the primary focus of a referral group.

Networking groups can be worthwhile if you are attentive. You will usually see a subset of people that attend the same meetings. Get to know those people. They have a commitment to networking and are candidates to become a center of influence or a pyramid capstone for you. I'll explain what these terms mean in a minute. Check in with the "regulars" at each meeting to stay connected, but don't linger too long with them. Move on to people you have never met before.

Always determine your objective for attending a networking meeting before you get there. Your objective may be different each time you go. Sometimes you may want to meet the maximum number of people you can; other times you may be looking for particular people or professions, or perhaps to make really quality connections with just a few new acquaintances. There is no single "right" goal for networking. The important thing is to have a goal every time you go to a meeting.

Referral group meetings are more structured. You are expected to be proactive in helping the other members in your referral group. You need to work to understand what a good referral is for them, and always be looking for opportunities to refer them. You also need to educate the other members on what is a good referral for you and give them the words that make it easy for them to refer others to you.

What do you mean by "give people the words that make it easy for them to refer others to you?"

Let me give you a specific example. I am a business coach. Members of my referral group told me they wanted to refer potential clients to me, but were afraid people would be insulted if they told them they could benefit from working with a business coach—it would be an indication of some perceived deficit in the other person.

I pointed out to my referral partners that the world's greatest golfer, Tiger Woods, has a coach. Why does the world's greatest golfer have a coach? Because he wants to get better and make more money. If the world's greatest can benefit from using a coach, can't the rest of us get better and make more money using a coach? This repositioned using a coach in their mind from remediation to maximizing already strong performance.

The Tiger Woods analogy worked in my situation. It won't work for everyone. You will need to create your own analogies or metaphors that will make it easy for people to give you referrals.

Is a referral group a good way to get more sales opportunities?

Yes. It's much more than that, though. The other members of your referral group enable you to broaden the portfolio of goods and services you can provide to clients and prospects. The quality of the people in your referral group allows you to offer more value to clients and prospects.

Let me give you an example. One of my clients called me from the airport on his way out of town to finalize the details of a proposal I was working on for him. He sounded a bit harried, so I asked him what was wrong. He told me that as he was getting ready to leave his home he had noticed a leak under a sink in his bathroom. He had to leave to catch his flight, so his wife had to handle it and she was having a hard time getting a plumber.

I asked my client if he would like my help getting a plumber that I trust, and by reference he could trust, too. He gratefully said yes. I contacted the plumber in my referral group, explained the situation, and asked him if he could juggle his schedule to fit in my customer that day.

He could, and he did. In that single transaction, my client got the help he needed to solve a problem, I solidified a client relationship, and the plumber in my group got a new customer. Talk about a win-win situation! This is the kind of synergy produced by "transformational networking." A strong network lets you help more people in more ways, enhancing their perception of your value.

Tell me more about referral groups.

There are a number of national organized referral groups with local chapters, like Le Tip, BNI, Gold Star Referral Clubs, Network Professionals, Inc. and others. Don't overlook regional or specialized organizations. In Central Ohio, an Ohio-based networking group called AmSpirit Business Connections has over 50 chapters, and many communities have groups that serve particular populations such as women or specific ethnicities.

Check around in your area to see who is active locally. Different organizations have different strengths and weaknesses, so shop around. Even different chapters of the same organization have different personalities; so visit a number of organizations and chapters until you find one where you feel right at home. One important thing to consider is the concept of a "core group": people in business categories that are synergistic with your business. For me, examples are: a business lawyer, an accountant, a payroll person, and people in other related business-to-business areas. For a real estate agent, good core group business categories would be an insurance person, a title company, a mortgage lender, a home inspector, a repairman, and other residential-related fields. Keep in mind that good synergies are about having customers in common, not necessarily about doing similar work. If your target customer is a corporate executive, try connecting to the tailor who makes his custom suits!

You said friends and acquaintances are other ways to network. What's the difference between friends and acquaintances?

The difference is in the strength of relationship ties. With friends you have strong ties. With acquaintances you have weak (or at least weaker) ties. But there is strength in weak ties. In his 1974 book *Getting a Job*, sociologist Mark Granovetter found that 56 percent of people found jobs through personal contacts.

Most people don't find this surprising. What IS surprising is that of those people who reported finding a job through personal contacts, 55.6 percent reported they saw their contact only occasionally, and 27.8 percent reported they saw their contact only rarely. So over 80 percent of jobs found through personal contacts come from contacts with weak ties.

Frank Agin gives a good treatment of this concept (and many more networking concepts, some of which I reference in this chapter) in his book *Foundational Networking: Building Know, Like, and Trust to Create a Lifetime of Extraordinary Success.*

What's a center of influence and a pyramid capstone?

A center of influence and a pyramid capstone are related concepts. A center of influence is a person, not necessarily a client, who knows a lot of people and is an influential advocate for you. They usually help you out of the goodness of their hearts. Find these people, cultivate them, keep them informed of your progress, and show gratitude to them on an ongoing basis.

A pyramid capstone is your power connector through whom you've met many people. You've probably heard the term "six degrees of separation", where any two people in the world can be connected by a chain of six people. This concept has been around for a long time, but it was reinforced by some experiments done in the 1960's by a social psychologist named Stanley Milgram.

Milgram gave some people in the Midwest the name and city of a person they did not know in New England, and asked them to try to get a letter to that person by forwarding it to someone they thought could help get the letter to the target. Of those letters that made it, it took on average about six steps to get the letter to the target.

But here's the surprise, and where the term pyramid capstone comes in. In one experiment, of the 24 letters that reached the target at his home, the same man gave 16 of them to the target person! Of those letters that reached the target at his office, more than half came from two other men.

Think about your connections. Most of your contacts became connected to you through a small number of well-connected people. You don't have a circle of friends; you have a collection of pyramids of friends you have met through a small number of people (pyramid capstones). To figure out who your pyramid capstones are, take a look at 40 of your friends and acquaintances (non-family), work backward through the chain of how you met them (I met Bob through Fred whom I met through Tom), and see if any common names emerge.

Those common names are your pyramid capstones. Cultivate these people. Keep meeting new people and develop some more pyramid capstones. Keep introducing people you know to people they don't know, and strive to become a pyramid capstone yourself. This is another aspect of transformational networking.

So it's kind of like the phrase "It's not what you know, it's who you know."

Yes, although it may be more accurate to say, "It's not who you know, it's who knows you." You only have influence to the extent that people know, like, and trust you.

OK, so a better way to say it is, "It's not who you know, it's who knows you."

Yes, but now that I think of it, it might be more accurate to say "It's not who knows you, it's who knows what you know."

Let's say you are a really good resource in a given area, but nobody knows it. Somebody can have a problem you could help them with, but they don't think to ask you because they don't realize you can help them. So an opportunity to help is lost.

How do you get around that?

I always ask what challenges people are facing, and I go out of my way to try to help them. I tell people that if they are ever looking for a solution to a problem, please let me know, even if it is not in an area they think of as my expertise. I want to be their go-to guy whenever they have a problem.

That's where the portfolio of goods and services represented by my referral group comes in. They enable me to help clients and prospective clients in a lot more ways than I can alone. If my immediate referral group can't help me or doesn't know someone who can help me, that's where all the business cards I collect at networking events come in handy. I scan my address book looking for people with the expertise needed to solve my client's problem.

If I find someone who can solve somebody else's problem, then I put them together. I can give a stronger endorsement if I have worked with the person before. If I have not worked with a person before, then I let the person with the problem know they need to exercise some due diligence before they retain the person I am referring.

What should we take away from this chapter?

Become the person you want to network with. Evaluate and refine your networking behaviors against that standard on an ongoing basis. Look for opportunities to help people, and to connect people to others who can help them. As you strive to become the person you want to network with, you will become a better networker—and a better person.

David Emery Smith is a business coach, public speaker, and the president of Performance Dynamics Systems. Dave helps professional people get clarity on the improved results they desire in their personal and professional lives, and works with them to develop and implement an action plan to get those results. Dave is certified in a number of personal and organizational assessment tools. He does one-on-one coaching, group coaching, and strategic planning.

Dave has a passion for adult learning and organizational development. He spent many years in sales force training and development with the Hewlett-Packard Company as part of this 25-year career there. He has two Masters degrees, one in Organizational Design and Effectiveness, and another in Human Development. One of his Master's theses was on using virtual learning environments in the corporate world. Dave combined his Master's thesis and the results of a pilot program he developed at Hewlett-Packard in a book chapter that was included in the Handbook of Online Learning (Sage Publications, 2002). Dave is also a highly rated adjunct professor at Franklin University in Columbus, Ohio, which focuses on adult learners.

In addition to his coaching business and his work as an adjunct professor, Dave is an Area Director with AmSpirit Business Connections. This networking group provides a venue for Dave to not only continually improve his own networking effectiveness, but also help other business professionals become more effective at networking.

David Emery Smith
Performance Dynamics Systems
2456 Powell Ave.
Columbus, OH 43209
614-946-4684
www.pdsystems.net
dsmith@pdsystems.net

CHAPTER FIVE

Micro-Marketing:
Big Results with a Small Budget

Dan Paulson, President/CEO, *InVision Business Development*

"The man who removes a mountain begins by carrying
away small stones."
—Chinese Proverb

What principle of selling has helped you be consistently successful?

Small businesses need others to know about them in order to succeed
and grow. As a small business owner you wear many different hats, none
more important than the "marketing" hat. You must build a strong brand
and make the most of limited time, money, and other marketing
resources. Effective marketing uses the brand that you have created to
draw others into a relationship with you and your business. In order for
your marketing to work, the brand you have created must differentiate
what you do from your competition.

Small business owners tend to think that generating revenues should
be easy. Behind this tendency is a basic belief. Small business owners

believe that they are really good at what they do. Since they are so good, everyone must know how good they are!

When business doesn't automatically flood through the doors, they look for an easy way of generating revenues. A critical and costly mistake ensues. Money, time and effort are thrown at "marketing". At this stage marketing usually consists of the following:

- A new logo
- A new brochure
- New letterhead
- A new advertising campaign

Lots of money is spent and when the return is measured – if it is ever measured – not much has happened. The business owner feels good because he or she has been doing something. However the real issue was missed – they never spent enough time developing and targeting the right message to the right audience.

How would I target the right message to the right audience?

Before you can explain to anyone else what you do, you must understand it yourself. You also need to understand what sort of customer is most likely to want and need what you do. Finally, you must be able to deliver what you promise. This can best be explained by using the three D's: **Define, Direct, and Deliver.**

Define – The Define step involves creating a clear vision for yourself and your business. This step requires creating a clear picture of your business so you can share that message with others. Failure to do so will cost you business.

To create a compelling vision, you must answer a number of questions. What does your business stand for? What do you ultimately hope to achieve for your clients? How is this clearly different from your competition? What do you want your business to become? Who is your target audience?

For example, imagine a printing company that spends all its energy telling you *what* they do. They are printers, aren't they? Don't most people who need those services already know what a printer does? Stating the obvious makes it hard for someone to distinguish why they should do business with one printer over another.

For the printer, the important questions to answer will be:

- "How do we define success?"
- "How do we look when we are successful?"
- "What makes our business different?"
- "Why should someone buy from us versus our competitors?"

Answering those questions brings clarity to the definition of the business.

Direct – Once you have defined your business, you need to direct it where to go. The process of defining should determine what type of clients are the best fit for your business. Completing this process will help you choose which prospects you want to pursue, and which others are not your ideal clients.

Here is a case in point. One of my clients was spending a large portion of their revenues on advertising. We analyzed where they were spending their money, and there was no strategy to it. Their money was spread out over multiple channels. Worse, their message didn't speak to any specific audience.

Their answer, when asked, was: "We can work with anyone. We don't want to limit ourselves." This philosophy was clearly backfiring, though; they had hardly any clients at all! In trying to speak to everyone, they created a message that didn't speak to anyone. They didn't have millions to invest in marketing, and so were unable to buy the frequency of ads they would need to get their message heard. By applying the "Define" and "Direct" steps to their marketing plan, they were able to develop a much clearer message that addressed their ideal target client. This greatly increased the effectiveness of their marketing, even as it reduced their marketing costs.

Deliver – In the end, you are only as good as your output. When you have defined who you are and directed that message to your audience, the only thing left is to deliver. Your most effective marketing tool is referrals from happy customers. After all, people expect *you* to make claims about your product or service. They are more impressed when *others* make those claims on your behalf.

Consider the case of a small dental practice who has been working with me over the past year and a half. In that time he was able to increase business in his already successful practice by over 28% in less than 12 months. So far he is tracking at 30% growth this year and erecting a new building to accommodate the business growth. He isn't going to be a small practice much longer.

The change? Prior to working together the dentist did not provide any unified direction. He worked well with his people – they liked him. They just didn't know what to do to help him make the practice more successful. The staff rarely met as a team. They had no idea where he wanted to take the practice or how their jobs might impact his plans.

He will testify that his present success is due to: a well-defined practice focus; a directed practice headed where he wants it to go; an engaged staff energized around a unified message; and service delivery that builds patient loyalty.

There are now daily meetings that:
- Review the prior day's events
- Allow the team to share what's planned for the day
- Remind the team why they are there – to build customer loyalty.

The rewards have been great. In addition to increasing his business, the dentist has also implemented an incentive plan for the performance of the team both individually and as a group. Each person has earned a raise; as much as $1000! Because the dentist is able to measure referrals and customer loyalty, it's a win-win.

How should I begin defining my business?

Defining your business means creating the thoughts and feelings that people get when either you or your business is mentioned. Think about popular brands like Disney and Coca-Cola. They create emotional triggers that link you to their brand. For example, the thought of Disney may have created an image in your head of Mickey Mouse or an experience you had at one of their theme parks. Based on your interaction with the brand, the feeling was either positive or negative.

When you market yourself or your business, you need to tap into these triggers as well. All purchasing decisions are emotional ones. People need a connection with the products and services they use. This becomes the differentiator for your business and goes far beyond the quality of product or service. You may have even experienced a time when you were able to prove your offering was better to a prospect, but they stayed with your competitor because of the relationship they had. The emotional trigger of that relationship was a stronger bond than the offering of a superior product.

Yet many businesses define themselves only by the attributes of their product or service. As a result, their message is very similar to that of their competitors. When prospective customers are investigating the market, they know little about the companies they are researching. The initial reaction is confusion. Subconsciously they look for that emotional connection to make the differentiation. Questions asked in this phase include: "Are the products or services a good fit for us?", "Does this company match my values and beliefs?" or "Is there someone that might be able to recommend them to me?" If a prospect is unsure or unable to find a differentiator, they will resort to comparing only on price. Once price is the differentiator, you have moved from unique product to commodity – a game that is hard to win and not very rewarding even if you do.

The best way to start defining your business is through your fans. Every business has a fan base. Your goal is to grow it. Talk to your devoutly loyal customers. They will help you understand why you are different from the rest. Your customers will also help you find the emotions you need to tap into, and what you need to communicate to find more like-minded people.

I encourage all business owners to create an advisory board to help them learn what they need to know. Invite colleagues you respect, clients, business partners and suppliers to a formal meeting to discuss your business and give you some direction. Ask questions like: "What separates my business from other competitors?" "What do you tell people about me and my company?" "What is the best way to find more people like you?" In a couple of hours you can uncover enough information to help define what separates you from the rest. You may even end up with referrals!

Why should I be looking for "like-minded people"?

Business leaders often think everyone who would have a need for their services is a prospect. To quote George Gershwin, "it ain't necessarily so." Even if your product does have the potential to reach a large audience, you still have to fill a unique need that is not currently being met. If you are a painter, plumber, banker, mechanic, or anyone else that is working in a competitive market, the chances that what you offer is truly different are slim.

Remember, people do business with people they know, like and trust. If you cannot fulfill all three for your prospect, they will not do business with you. Accept the fact that you are not going to do business with everyone. Instead, focus on those who share the same interests that you do. This gives you an advantage because you know what's important to them and where you can find them. You can go directly to them with your marketing. This more targeted approach attracts business to you much more effectively and efficiently.

Once I have the message and know who to reach out to, how do I do it?

This involves **Directing** your message to your audience. The better you know WHO you are trying to reach, the easier it will be for you to know WHERE you need to put that message. Networking is one great way to get your message out, and my colleague, David Smith, devotes a whole chapter of this book just to that topic. For purposes of our discussion here, I want to focus on *where* to network.

When I started my business I went to as many networking events as I could. I was new in business and still trying to figure out what my business was all about. I soon discovered that I was wasting a lot of time. When I understood who my prospects were, I realized they weren't at the events I was attending. I wanted to meet business owners, presidents, and CEOs. Instead, I was meeting mid-level employees or sales reps that were not the key decision-makers in their companies. Sometimes these contacts could help me but most times they could not. I determined that if I wanted to meet CEOs and business owners, I had to find out where they were and how they networked. This led to a targeted approach to networking and meetings.

A word of caution: being directed is more than simply networking. You can waste a lot of time and money to reach your prospects. Once you understand the kind of business you want, you will determine the best balance to get it. Advertisers are more than happy to take your money and tell you that their method is the best. Whether it is web, print, TV or radio, the costs may outweigh the benefits.

Soft costs are important as well. You may call them opportunity costs. Supposedly "free" marketing tactics like social media, writing and networking can eat up your time.   Instead of giving up money directly you are giving up time. Always ask yourself, "What could I be doing right now to make a difference in the direction of my business?" If you are **Directed**, you know who to reach and you will limit activities that will not place you in front of your prospect.

What should I do once I have Defined and Directed my business?

There are many options, and you have to determine what is going to be right for you.   Some businesses get good results using traditional marketing methods, such as phone book ads, websites, radio, newspaper, magazine ads, television and billboards. What you will find about each of these methods is they can be expensive and difficult to measure in terms of return on your investment.

The better you understand your target audience, the more you can reduce your expenses and get greater results. Each situation is different. For example, I would typically avoid Yellow Page ads because they do not work for me. However, I know of companies that have great success with the Yellow Pages. One owns an independent insurance agency in a small town. Many of their customers are older farmers. Because their focus is geographically local, and many of their target customers rely on the yellow pages as their main resource for finding services, they have great success with phone book ads.   By contrast, the insurance agency next door might choose to target international business travelers. They would likely have no luck with the local Yellow Pages, but might do very well with ads in airline in-flight magazines.

If you're not sure how your customers find the services they need, ask! As you look for business, ask your prospects how their industry communicates. Seek to learn from your target market, and once you know where they are, make sure you are there with them.

What is the best type of marketing tactic to use?

The best marketing approach for you is the one that gets the results you want. Notice, it is about getting the results *you* want, not what other businesses want. Every business is different. Since results are key, whatever you do to market yourself, be sure it is measurable. How else will you know if it is working?

A prospect of mine was struggling with sales in his company. They had done some limited advertising without much luck. As the owner watched sales continue to fall, he decided he had to do something about it. What was his solution? Advertise more! He had been sold on frequency. The pitch was: "More ads means more people see them, and when more people see the ads, more people will shop." It sounds perfectly logical to expect more sales with greater exposure. In this case, though, it didn't happen. In fact, nothing changed and sales still declined.

Activity does not equal productivity. The many thousands of dollars this company spent on marketing went nowhere because they didn't know who their audience was. They had two problems: lack of direction and failure to measure. Measuring their responses would have revealed that the increase in marketing activity was not producing results. Once you know something is not working, you can make the necessary changes to get the results you want. Feedback of all kinds is essential – you can't succeed in a vacuum.

You have suggested getting feedback from your clients and prospects. Does that really help?

YES! It shows that you are actively seeking to address the needs of your target audience. As I suggested before, an advisory board is a wonderful tool for accomplishing this. Let me be more specific. An advisory board is a group of six to ten people that you solicit to help you in your business. The group should be comprised of your centers of influence, current clients and prospects. Invite people you know and trust.

Invite your group to attend an initial two-hour session. The purpose of the session is to help provide direction for your business and review your marketing messages. When you meet as a group, explain that you would like their help to understand how to reach your target audience. By soliciting input, you will learn what they are looking for and how to communicate. In the process you may also get referrals and possibly business!

There is a lot of discussion today about social media. Is that a good option for marketing a business?

Depending on your business model and target audience, it might be a great option. First, let's define social media in relation to traditional media. Traditional media is anything that you "push" to prospects. Examples include print, television and radio. It may also include static websites. Push media tends to be non-specific, intrusive and based on assumptions about what your clients want. Traditional media such as television and radio send information out. In effect they choose what information you see or hear.

Social media is a "pull" method, meaning the consumer gets the choice of what information to gather. Your goal with social media is to get people to follow you – to want your content. With the advent of the Internet and other high-speed, easy-to-use communication technologies, the end user can now choose what content they get and how much, based on their own interests and needs.

Social media has led to online networking. Online networking starts with building an online community, and then populating that community with people you know or want to know. Social media sites like MySpace, Facebook, LinkedIn and Twitter have become immensely popular in the last few years. Large networks of "friends" or contacts have been built, enabling people to get connected not only to many new acquaintances, but also to people from their past experiences, previous jobs and schools. How might your business benefit if all of your old coworkers or classmates knew what you are doing now?

The number of people participating in online networking communities is in the millions. Social networking allows us to interact with people and the communities in which they participate in a whole new way. When there is that much buzz and that kind of concentration of potential clients in one place, businesses small and large want to take advantage of it. Few businesses understand how to capitalize on the new media. Those that do will have a competitive advantage.

People want to connect with content in much the same way they connect with others. By connecting with content, they feel a sense of ownership. The challenge for business is to develop information in new ways and find the right way to disseminate it to the right target audience. Information needs to be packaged differently.

Once you determine how to present your business in the world of social media, the possibilities are literally endless. The boundaries of your business can stretch well beyond the city in which you live. You are no longer limited by geography to sell products or services. Building relationships online may require a different way of working from what you are used to, but it can be done. In such an environment, DEFINE, DIRECT and DELIVER become even more important. Because the opportunities are limitless, so is the opportunity for distraction.

How would I participate on an individual basis in an online community?

While there are individual site differences, the common purpose of the majority of communities is to build relationships. The first step is to create a profile for visitors to view. Your profile will contain information about you, your business, background and contact information. Some sites allow pictures and others do not.

The more information you have posted, the easier it is for others to find you, so try to include enough information to make your profile unique to you. Use common sense, though – unique identifiers such as birth date, home address or ID numbers could invite identity theft. If you wouldn't be comfortable giving a particular bit of personal information to a group of total strangers, it probably doesn't belong in your social media profile. A professional photo of you is a great choice; photos of your kids may not be appropriate.

When others do find you, they have a chance to view your profile and connect with you. There are myriad reasons for creating a connection. It is your choice whether to accept an invitation.

There are two schools of thought about building a network. Both approaches have advantages and disadvantages. The first approach is to link only with people you know. The size of your network will depend on your face-to-face connections and your ability to network with people you know. The advantages of this kind of network include reliability, greater security and depth of relationship. The downside is that your network is limited by physical connection. Should you decide to use this networking philosophy, you will be marketing to people you already know.

The second way is to be an "open" networker. Open networkers build very large networks of people that they may never meet or interact with in any other way than being connected to them. The advantages of open networking are reach, greater potential for interaction and bragging rights for building a large network. The downsides are lack of relationship depth and time spent maintaining the network.

Can you be more specific? What sites are out there and how can I access them?

There are as many online communities as there are areas of human interest. Think of every cause or group that you can and there will be an online community for it. Your decisions whether to get involved will depend on your market focus and your areas of interest. There are some basic sites, though, that have the widest audiences and therefore, the widest appeal. I have outlined those sites and how to access them below.

One word of caution before we go further – social media and online networking can be very time consuming. Building, maintaining and participating actively in this medium takes a lot of effort. Should you decide to market using these media, the decision must be made as a part of your overall media and marketing strategy. Otherwise there is significant risk that you will waste a lot of time and accomplish little.

When you make the decision to get involved in social media, here are a few venues that you should consider:

LinkedIn: www.linkedin.com

LinkedIn was originally designed for HR departments, recruiters and job seekers. Since then, it has expanded into an excellent way to network, collaborate, and get business. LinkedIn works on the premise that everyone on earth is only six points of contact away from knowing everyone else. LinkedIn is becoming an essential tool for relationship management and marketing.

LinkedIn has a free service and a pay component. Basic membership is free and most of its features are available at no cost. There are monthly subscription packages that vary in cost and accessibility. For instance, one level allows you to perform deeper searches of the on-line network. Another level allows better connectivity and messaging with other LinkedIn members.

Once you become a member, begin building a contact list on the site. To do so, search for people you know who are already members. Then, download your list of contacts and invite them to join your network. People who are directly connected to you are called your "first degree" connections. The people to whom they are connected are your "second degree," and so on.

One of the benefits of membership is the ability to be introduced to others in the network by your connections. Search for people you would like to meet and look for a chain of connections between you and them. LinkedIn helps you manage the series of contact messages – you send a message to someone you know, they send to someone they know, and so on until your target is reached. This can be a great way to get a referral.

LinkedIn does not limit the number of connections you can have. However, the site does request that you only invite people you know. They do police it. When you receive an invitation to link, you have three choices. You may accept the invitation, archive it and take no action or you may click "I don't know this person". If you click "I don't know..." LinkedIn is notified. Should you receive five "I don't knows..." you will be barred from sending any more invitations without appealing to LinkedIn administrators.

One other way of creating interest in you is to join interest groups on LinkedIn. There are alumni groups, sales groups, recruiting groups, and geographic groups – just about any kind of group you can imagine. LinkedIn allows you to join up to 25 groups. As a member you can post questions and respond to questions posted by others. By doing so you have the opportunity to link with like-minded people and develop a broader network.

Plaxo: www.plaxo.com

Plaxo started life as an online address book utility. It shares a lot of similarities with LinkedIn. It is primarily a business network that allows business people to connect directly and through groups. Plaxo differs from LinkedIn in the type of information it shares. Plaxo readily shares contact data with others in your network. Think of it as an online business card.

Plaxo is good for keeping your contact information up to date. There are various ways to connect to others, and you can participate in groups and forums much like other social networks. Plaxo also has an interesting feature that is helpful in building relationships. Because you are able to list birthday information, you can receive a notice when one of your contacts is having a birthday. Plaxo has a neat e-card system that allows you to choose a card to send to that individual on their birthday. You can set up notification alerts well in advance of the special day so you can have the card sent at the right time.

Plaxo is a free membership. You may purchase upgrades for a nominal annual fee. The biggest benefit of paying for membership is to be able to choose from a larger selection of e-cards to send. Plaxo limits the number of contacts you can have in your database to one thousand. For this reason, Plaxo is better used for closer or longer-term relationships rather than the "open networking" strategy that might cause your database to exceed the size limit.

Facebook: www.facebook.com

Facebook tends to be used as a casual social networking site. While you may have business connections on Facebook, you will also probably find friends and family connecting to you. From a business vantage point Facebook is more about getting people to know you as an individual. It may not bring you the type of contacts you are looking for. You are more likely to find old high school classmates or friends from other parts of your life here.

On the personal side, Facebook provides entertainment value. The demographic skews older than other social networking sites – the average age of members is 47 as of May 2009. Besides networking, there are hundreds of third party applications that can keep you entertained, or distracted. You may find yourself bogged down while responding to requests from connections to have a virtual "drink" or take the latest relationship quiz.

It can still be beneficial to you and your business to be a member and pay attention to Facebook. It gives people the chance to know you as a person and understand your business. As we go to press with this book,

Facebook is free, and that will probably continue to be the case at least for the near future.

There are several good applications for posting weblog entries (discussed later in this chapter) and Twitter information to Facebook, so this site allows you to combine both business and personal activities. Be cautious, though – because of its highly social nature you will want to monitor the content on your Facebook page closely. Friends can link pictures and content that may not be representative of your business or the professional image you want to present at this time. The party picture that your buddy thinks is funny may end up costing you business.

Twitter: www.twitter.com

Twitter is a service that allows you to share thoughts and experiences in 140 characters or less. This is called "micro-blogging." The purpose of Twitter is to build a database of followers who monitor your activity or "tweets." It is a great tool for sharing your thoughts, posting articles, giving your followers updates, and linking to content. Because of Twitter's instantaneous delivery of your message to your followers, it is great for getting the word out quickly. If you have a large network, you can get immediate responses to questions and thoughts.

Twitter may be used for everything from connecting with your followers to broadcasting information, from making announcements to sharing general thoughts of the day. Some people comment about very mundane things such as driving to work or getting a haircut. Others are very targeted and focus on getting a specific marketing message out. A targeted use is to connect people to a blog and make announcements about speaking engagements and seminars.

YouTube: www.youtube.com

YouTube is a site for online video sharing. You can use YouTube to post video content to an account you create. From a business standpoint, this is a great way to get people to understand your product or service.

The idea is to post content that people would want to view and pass along to their network. How-to videos posted on the site by you may educate prospects about your business. To be the most effective, the content must be meaningful, valuable and entertaining. An online commercial will attract viewers ONLY if it has high entertainment value. YouTube is a free service.

You have mentioned "blogs". What are they and how can you use them to market?

The term "blog" is short for "weblog". Weblogs are exactly what you'd expect: logs on the web. In other words, a blog is an online diary. To begin a blog, create an account on any of the many websites that host blogs. Then post to your blog. Blogs give the world a chance to read your thoughts and ideas. One feature of a blog is its interactive nature. If your content is interesting enough, others will enjoy reading it. Readers can also post direct comments on your entries and link to your blog to follow the content.

There are some tactics you can use to get the word out about your blog. The best way is to connect to other blogs. Find out who is well recognized for writing content similar or complementary to your own, and regularly make comments on their blogs. Link your comments back to your own blog. This thread will attract people to see what you are writing about. A blog that already has lots of followers will provide the greatest opportunity to expand your network.

Another way to expand your blog is to push your content to other networks. In LinkedIn, you can create a connection to your blog that people can directly view without leaving the LinkedIn site. Post a "tweet" on Twitter to announce an updated blog. Don't just make one announcement and feel you have reached your audience. It is important to make many announcements throughout the day. People with large networks may not see your first announcement so if you broadcast only once, you may not get the visibility you want.

Tie your blog into your website to create more value. By doing so and posting faithfully to your blog, search engines will have an easier time finding your site. You will need to write a minimum of one blog post every other day to be truly effective.

It seems like social media can be a big waste of time. How do people get business out of it?

Social media can indeed be a huge waste of time. You have to be very clear about your purpose in using it. Social media is about creating awareness and building your fan base. Your activity in social media can help people learn about you online. Your goal is to build awareness and connect with people who share the same interests, values and beliefs.

The key is that people decide to connect with you. You aren't "pushing" to your connections; they are "pulling" you to them. The more this loyal following grows, the greater the opportunity to have your information passed along. Social media provides an outlet for you to continually share your message with your followers. Over time, your followers will come to you when they have a need.

Social media is also great for spreading your message quickly. The larger your following, the greater the opportunity to monetize those relationships. This book is a good example. I told my followers it was available through my online resources. You may even be reading it because you learned about it in this way. I was able to share short excerpts in several online venues to gain interest and sell copies. Eventually the book and my online content will lead to a new business contact and more revenue.

How do you go about leveraging those relationships?

First, determine which social media outlets you want to participate in. Limit your participation to three or four networks unless you can find tools that will allow you to share information seamlessly across multiple networks.

Next, start your network with the people who already know you. Take LinkedIn for example. After you start your membership, invite your friends and business connections to join. Invite them to build their networks. As people add to their network, yours expands as well. By checking weekly updates, you can see who is coming into your network. When you see people you would like to add to your network, use your connections to get an introduction to them. This allows you to contact them directly. When you contact people through your extended network, you create the opportunity to sell to them.

In what ways do you interact with your network?

There are many ways, from micro-blogging (very short informational messages) to discussion groups. Many sites such as LinkedIn, Facebook and Twitter ask you what you are doing at that moment. The premise is to give short, concise messages that will generate interest. You could talk about an online article you just wrote, or a speech you are writing for a seminar. Whatever it may be, it can help people understand what you do.

Discussion groups are a little different. These groups are where people of similar interests come together to ask/answer questions, collaborate, and inform. They can exist by themselves, as part of a networking site like LinkedIn or Facebook, or as part of a business or special interest website. You could even create a discussion group on your own website. Because people voluntarily join these groups, they already have an interest in the subject matter. They provide a great opportunity to reach an audience that wants to hear what you have to say. The best way to participate in these groups is to ask and answer questions. Your responses are usually posted for everyone to see. This helps establish expertise as well as raise questions that may generate interest in what you do. Find the online communities where you can share what you are passionate about.

Is there anything else I should be doing to market my business?

Nurture marketing is the last piece of the marketing puzzle. Nurture marketing is keeping in contact with prospects and clients through regular "touches." For example, a newsletter is a wonderful way of keeping in touch with people and educating them about you and your business. It requires a little work but the payoffs can be huge. If you are not good at writing, there are services that will put together a newsletter for you for a fee. This will save time and the worry of what to write about. I think of my newsletter as a reflection of my business and an opportunity to share my thoughts, so I take the time to write my own. Newsletters and other regular communications nurture your relationships and keep your name at the top of your customers' minds.

However you choose to do it, it is important to maintain a continuous stream of information. While this may not pay off immediately, it will secure business for you down the road as it maintains top-of-mind awareness.

If you had to summarize some key points, what would they be?

Small business success is all about exposure. You have an advantage over larger companies because you can be more resilient and respond faster to the changing dynamics of your market. The key is to understand which marketing opportunities fit your strategy and will get the results you want.

Remember: strategy first. Make sure you clearly understand who you are and what you do. If you don't, you can be sure no one else will. Be concise in how you communicate your message and make sure everyone in your organization is on board.

Be sure to follow the three D's: **Define, Direct, and Deliver.**

- **Define** your business, goals and target audience.
- **Direct** your focus to that audience for maximum benefit.
- **Deliver** on what you promise. The best marketing is a referral.

Remember, you are in a relationship business. Spend your time building relationships through the channels of networking, traditional marketing and social media. Work your plan and you will be successful!

Daniel Paulson is President/CEO of InVision Business Development and a strategist, executive coach, writer, and public speaker. He holds Certified Business Coach and Attribute Index certifications. Dan works internationally with CEOs, Boards of Directors, and business professionals to develop the skills necessary to become world-class organizations that deliver on performance, profitability, and customer loyalty.

He has written for Business Watch, several trade publications, and actively blogs about current events in business. Dan's "Biz Bits" online monthly newsletter is recognized for its short, on-point messages about business success. He has collaborated on previous books and will release his first solo work, "Apples to Apples," in late 2009.

Dan founded InVision Business Development in 2005 to help leaders address challenges with people, planning and process. He recognized early in his career that strategic plans often fail due to poor communication and improper alignment to the Vision of the company, and now successfully guides organizations past those challenges to greater success. He speaks nationally on the subjects of strategy, leadership, sales and customer loyalty.

Active in community projects, Dan works with local chambers of commerce to help small businesses grow and prosper. He is actively involved in Downtown Madison, Inc. and has served on the advisory boards for Techskills and Madison Media Institute. He currently serves on the board of directors for With Wings and a Halo, a not-for-profit dedicated to supplying books and backpacks to emergency workers to give to children affected by traumatic events.

Dan Paulson

InVision Business Development
P.O. Box 45920
Madison, WI 53744
608-235-5320

www.invisionbusinessdevelopment.com
dan@invisionbusinessdevelopment.com

CHAPTER SIX

Sell What the Client is Buying

Tracy Lunquist, President, *Working Magic*

"Listening is such a simple act. It requires us to be present, and that takes practice, but we don't have to do anything else. We don't have to advise, or coach, or sound wise. We just have to be willing to sit there and listen."
—Margaret J. Wheatley

What principle of selling has helped you be consistently successful?

To me, the most important "selling principle" is not a selling principle at all — it's a basic human principle. Before you will buy from me, you have to trust me and believe you will gain value from doing business with me. So if I want you to buy from me, I have to understand who you are and what you are buying, regardless of what I am selling. I need to be attentive, interested, and in tune with your agenda. This human principle of paying attention and caring genuinely for others leads naturally to the successful selling principle of selling what the client wants to buy.

It's remarkable how often someone will get into "selling" mode and, in the words of my very successful colleague Michael Sleppin, "will try to sell a blue hat to a lady who's shopping for red shoes." Wouldn't it be easier, and more satisfying for both salesperson and customer, to sell her red shoes?

There are lots of ways we get off the client's agenda, and they usually boil down to self-centeredness, or self-consciousness. It's true in any sales situation, but especially so in service professions like consulting, coaching, and health care – it's not about you, it's about the client. The more anxious you get about whether you look good, sound good, have all the answers, or can fit the client into the mold of a particular product you want to sell, the further you stray from what's really important.

What *is* really important?

Your client's wants and needs are the most important thing in a sales meeting. *Period.* You can't sell anything to anyone until you know what they want to buy, and you won't know what they're buying until you know what problems they are trying to solve. To learn the answers to these questions, first you must ask, and then you must listen.

One of the toughest challenges I had to overcome as a salesperson was to *stop talking.* When I'm meeting with a client, my goal is to understand their situation. Only when I understand their wants and needs can I move into "matchmaker" mode, looking for a good fit between the services I offer and the needs they have expressed. It's common sense, really – if I want to understand someone, I need to be listening to them, not talking. A great way to remember this is to use the acronym WAIT – which stands for, "Why Am I Talking?"

Of course, your own goals are also important. Fortunately, if you are talking to the right client, your goals and theirs will be quite compatible.

How will I know I'm talking to the right client?

You can, and should, do your homework before you go into a meeting with a prospective client. You want to meet with people who have a need for your product and who have the ability to make a purchase decision. My colleagues have talked about networking, prospecting and marketing in other chapters of this book, and I encourage you to use that great information to develop a strategy to find the right customers for your business.

In the final analysis, though, you will know you are talking to the right client when the conversation reveals that your goals are compatible. Their goal is to get their needs met, and your goal is to earn their business by meeting those needs. When your offering and your client's needs intersect to your mutual benefit, you are highly likely to make a sale and enter a mutually satisfying professional relationship. Remember this: you will only discover that magical intersection of everyone's priorities if you're really paying attention.

What if you're listening, but the client isn't talking?

Good question. And as it happens, "good questions" are the answer. The purpose of any sales meeting is to build trust and to discover what the client needs. Asking the right questions can accomplish both. Your initial questions should build a respectful and insightful foundation. Questions like, "How did you get into this business?" or "What are some of your organization's greatest strengths?" establish rapport and demonstrate that you really care about your client. At the same time, they encourage him or her to start opening up to you.

The client's willingness to talk honestly with you will indicate that it's safe to dig a little deeper. When you sense you have that permission, you might explore topics such as goals the client hopes to achieve, and obstacles standing in their way. As you continue to build rapport, you can explore slightly riskier questions, like "Tell me more about what's getting in the way of achieving your goal?" or "If you had to place a dollar value on that obstacle, what would it be?" For example, if the client has said that high employee turnover is a problem, ask specifically, "How much do you think high employee turnover is costing your organization?" Pay close attention to body language and how the client reacts to your questions. Back off or try a different approach if you're getting short or noncommittal answers, or if the client seems guarded or uncomfortable. Remember, your goal is to build trust – and by that, I mean real trust, not just the illusion of it.

I cannot overemphasize that this is not a game. Your goal is not simply to convince someone you care about them if you don't. Your clients don't all need to be your best friends, but if you are more interested in taking their money than you are in solving their problem, no amount of clever selling technique is going to make a bit of difference. You can use the "As Seen on TV" approach for selling products whose commitment point is relatively low, but if you are seeking a long-term relationship in which you provide a valuable service to a loyal customer, you must possess a real desire to help them.

What do you mean by "commitment point," and the "As Seen on TV approach"?

Commitment point is to a service relationship as "price point" is to a product on a store shelf. When we talk about professional services, cost is not the only, or even the most important consideration for many clients. As a business coach, I ask a prospective client to commit not only their dollars, but also their time and personal energy to the process of professional development. The client absolutely must trust me, believe the process will work for them, and be prepared to commit many hours of concentrated time and effort to our work together. The same could be said of a patient's commitment to work with a doctor to treat his cancer, or a client's commitment to work through an estate plan with her attorney.

A box of cookies on a store shelf carries a low commitment point. I can throw it into my grocery cart, pay a few dollars, and consume it at my leisure. A cell phone has a slightly higher commitment point. I have to learn how to use a particular phone's features, pay a higher price, and typically enter into a multi-year contract. Most of the services being provided by readers of this book will likely have a high commitment point, involving potentially thousands of dollars of financial investment as well as significant time and effort on the part of the client. A sales process that will work at the "box of cookies" commitment point, will probably not be sufficient to persuade a client at the "estate plan" or "cancer treatment" commitment point.

I'm using the phrase "As Seen on TV approach" to describe the classic cable TV commercial formula, where you see the black and white image of the frustrated consumer clumsily operating some sort of outmoded tool, followed by a glorious full-color presentation of the fabulous new product that will magically and economically solve all of your problems for "three easy payments of $19.99 – but wait, there's more! Act now and we'll double the offer!"

What is interesting about those commercials is that they use the same basic sales process taught and coached by every author in this book, just in a very oversimplified way. The basic steps of identifying a problem, offering a solution and finding a fit are all presented in a neat and tidy 60-second package. The differences are in the prospecting step and in the method of finding fit. In the prospecting step, the TV commercial relies on reaching a huge audience rather than targeting the most likely prospects. In the "matchmaking" step, the commercial promotes the product and seeks to find a fit with the client, whereas a professional service provider centers on the client and seeks to find a fit with the product.

The "As Seen on TV" approach also tends to emphasize a price point or other economic argument as its primary value proposition. I would not recommend this approach for any reader of this book. As a provider of a professional service, you will have much greater success focusing on your expertise, excellent service, or customized solutions as your value proposition, rather than price.

Interesting – it hadn't ever occurred to me to deconstruct one of those commercials before.

You can learn a lot about sales by watching how other people do it, and evaluating how well their techniques work. The TV commercial formula would not be nearly as prevalent as it is, if it didn't work extremely well. Because you know this formula is effective, it is worthwhile to examine it and try to learn why that is the case.

By contrast, I'm sure you've had a terrible experience with a salesperson at some point in your life. What it was about that experience that turned you off? Did you not care for the salesperson's attitude? Did you feel uncomfortable or pressured? Reflecting on those experiences will help you figure out what *not* to do when you're the one doing the selling!

May we come back to what we were talking about before, about building rapport and trust with the client?

Absolutely. This is another key difference between the professional services sales process vs. the "As Seen on TV" formula. Most TV commercials emphasize the product – features, quality, price, or brand. A service professional may not have a "product" at all. In my business, for example, my "product" is defined by my client, in the form of business results they want to achieve by working with me. As a service professional you are not selling a product, you are selling yourself. More to the point, you are not selling your qualifications and technical expertise; *you are selling your ability to solve the client's problem.*

A common mistake service professionals make in the sales meeting is to talk too much about how they do what they do. This confuses the prospect and disrupts the process of building rapport and trust. Your doctor doesn't start by showing you all her surgical instruments or the Physician's Desk Reference book, and you'd be flummoxed if she did. Computer people can be especially guilty of presenting extensive, brilliant and bewildering descriptions of their services. You may be certain your client does not understand, nor care, exactly how you will fix a broken computer. The questions they need answered are how soon will it be fixed, and how can you prevent this from happening again?

Your conversation with the client will lead to a sale if, and *only* if, the client is convinced that you are the right person to help them get the results they are looking for. When you demonstrate, by asking good questions and paying attention to the client's answers, that you are really on their agenda, your client will come to trust you.

How will I know if the meeting is going well?

If you are paying attention, you can tell if someone is comfortable or not. The meeting is going well if the client is open to you. They are making eye contact, answering your questions in a thoughtful way, and showing signs of engagement in the conversation. Depending on the nature of your questions, your client may or may not be comfortable or relaxed, but their answers will tell you they trust you. If you are asking them questions about a problem they are having, they may seem nervous or even angry. Don't panic! You'll know by their answers and by their body language whether that discomfort is related to the problem they are discussing, or to their feelings about you. If you've ever had a friend confide in you about a troubling issue, then you know what it looks like when someone is upset by a situation as compared to being upset *with you.*

Body language is important, but read it in the context of the situation. I may frown when I'm thinking, or cross my arms because I'm cold. Those gestures do not necessarily mean I am upset or disagreeing with you.

Conversely, I might smile right before I stand up and escort you out of my office! Context matters.

In some selling situations you may fully intend for the client to be somewhat uncomfortable. This approach is sometimes called "finding the prospect's pain." If you are pursuing this course, pay close attention to what the client is saying, and what they are not saying. If your client seems to be evading a question, changing the subject, or volleying (tossing a question back to you), you may need to find a different tack to take. If they are uncomfortable, but are responding to your questions openly and honestly, you're probably on the right track.

Tell me more about "finding pain." Do I need to find the client's pain in order to make a sale?

You want to discover their wants and needs. If their need is related to a problem that is costing them time, money, or other resources, or is making life unpleasant in some way, your discovery process will find some "pain." Discovering that kind of pain may be advantageous to you, because a client experiencing that will tend to be motivated to buy a solution they believe will fix the problem.

However, the poor guy doesn't need to be bleeding on his desk in order for you to reach a deal. Buying is absolutely an emotional process – that's true in every case. But a client is just as likely to buy to gain benefits, such as saving money or improving productivity, as to avoid consequences. Your goal is to help the client. The particulars of that are going to be unique to each situation.

The key, as I've said previously, is to be on the client's agenda. I occasionally see salespeople do something that strikes me as terribly disingenuous and disrespectful of the client. It's a misinterpretation of the "hurt and rescue" approach to selling. The short version of this approach is: find the client's pain (hurt) and then provide the solution to it (rescue). In one unfortunate variation of this approach, the salesperson, finding no apparent pain, feels compelled to create some.

A case in point was a gentleman who came to my door selling security systems. I politely declined his offer, and he walked away, shaking his head, saying, "Okay, good luck, hope nothing happens to you." Not only did this show of false empathy completely fail to interest me in his product, it caused me to wonder if he was actually a burglar posing as a security system salesman as a way of "casing" the neighborhood. If the goal of a sales meeting is to build rapport and trust, I think we can safely say this meeting was a spectacular failure!

To me, this is the key difference between a "sales guy" and a professional who sells. A "sales guy" goes through the motions of building trust and finding a fit, but in reality is just contriving a problem that his product solves and hoping the client doesn't catch on until the check is signed. A professional works to build a real relationship in which both client and service provider experience genuine value. Executives, entrepreneurs, and business owners will be much more successful when they apply the same level of professionalism to the sales process as they do to their areas of primary expertise.

Are you saying that one of the ways we can be more successful at sales is not to behave like salespeople?

Not exactly. I think it's worth clarifying here that if you're doing all the things you should be doing in a client meeting, you'll be much too busy to do any of the things you shouldn't be doing. I think we get bogged down as non-sales people when we get this idea that "sales" is some sort of entirely different mode of being from normal human existence. You can pick up the phone and invite a friend or a colleague to lunch, but somehow picking up the phone to make a "sales call" feels different. It shouldn't. The only difference between a sales meeting and any other kind of meeting is your goal for the meeting.

As a business owner, you know the value of time, so you'd never hold any kind of meeting without a clear purpose in mind, right? In the case of a sales meeting, the purpose is to seek a mutually beneficial business relationship with the client. Of course, you could say that the purpose of almost any meeting is to seek, create, or nurture a mutually beneficial business relationship, so even on that count, a sales meeting is not much different from any other kind of meeting. I think it's helpful to remind yourself of that as you go into the meeting. If at any time you feel like it's going off the rails, take a moment to refocus on that goal before you move on.

What else can I do to feel more comfortable in a sales meeting?

Relax, for starters. Before you ever go into a client meeting, take a moment to connect to your own passion for what you do, and your genuine interest in this client. Connect to yourself, so you're not tempted to try to be somebody else when you're in the meeting. The you that sells is not a different person from the you that does your main work, which in turn isn't really a different person from the you that loves your family, drives your car or pursues your hobbies. Personal integrity is absolutely key. The more at peace you are with yourself, the more you can leave your ego behind and open yourself up to understanding your client.

In service professions, the thing we're calling "selling" is really matchmaking. It's finding the right fit between you and your client – creating the business relationship that provides maximum value for both of you. Once you have that goal in mind, the conversation becomes not only more comfortable, but also more professional.

Another thing that can help you with confidence and focus is to take notes. Jotting down key items as they come up in the conversation does three things. One, it shows that you are engaged and serious about what your client is saying. Two, it helps you process the information by sending it through more than one mental pathway. And three, it documents important points you may want to revisit later in the discussion, and in subsequent meetings.

What are some other ways I can build credibility with prospective clients?

Start by building your credibility within yourself. Not only are you a top-notch sales professional; *you are a CEO.* It's important to see yourself in that light when you go into a client meeting. You are a peer to the person you are meeting, with equal expertise, credibility, and value to bring to the table. Your business cards say "President" or "CEO" or "Owner" – and if they don't, they should – so don't be afraid to live that role and feel good about doing so.

When you see yourself as a CEO, several wonderful things happen:

- You will feel confident meeting with the CEO of the client company, and comfortable expecting to be directed "straight to the top".

- CEOs and owners operate at a strategic level rather than a tactical level. They think in terms of big picture and strategic business outcomes. When you think and act like a CEO, you will naturally align your solutions with the strategic needs of your client's company, rather than giving a "sales pitch."

- CEOs and owners typically don't have budgets. When you and your peer CEO are discussing solutions, you can have total confidence that no one else's permission is needed to move forward with a deal, and you both have the flexibility to create the relationship that addresses all of the key issues.

- It is always easier to be referred down than to be referred up. Even if your solution is not meant to be implemented at the CEO level, it can certainly be chosen there.

Once I have established credibility as a peer to my client, what's next?

We know the goal of the meeting is to forge a mutually beneficial business relationship. If things are going well, the client is talking freely about what a successful outcome looks like to them. Now you're ready to focus the dialog on whether, and if so how, your service will fit their needs. As an executive peer to your client, you are "matchmaking," not selling. You are looking for points of connection, where the client's challenges and opportunities align with the services you offer. Ideally you have something in your menu of services that will help them achieve more than one of their goals – for example, improving their customer service while also reducing their costs. Even if you can help them achieve just one of their high priority goals, the client is likely to appreciate what you are offering.

As you have this conversation, keep two things in mind. First, be careful not to rush the fact-finding process. If you leap for a sale at the first hint of a fit, you may be missing some additional information that would lead to a better sale. For example, suppose your company offers a variety of staffing services, including human resources compliance and payroll processing. You are meeting with a client who mentions that she is not happy with her payroll department's performance, and you immediately go into your "pitch" about how outsourcing payroll will reduce her costs and improve service. You get the contract for payroll processing, only to discover later that one of your biggest competitors has a multimillion dollar contract to provide workers' compensation, safety training, employee benefits and travel services. Did the client even know you offer those other services? Could they have saved a bundle by going with your company for all of them? Will either of you ever know?

Not only will you sell more by being patient and accurate in your diagnosis, you'll also look smarter doing it. Playing out the scenario above, imagine going to a subsequent client meeting to say, "Hey! We do this stuff too, and could save you money!" It may work, but more likely it will be met with skepticism: "Why are you only bringing this up now?" You've essentially just proven that you are more interested in selling a product than in building a relationship.

The second, closely related item is to watch out for assumptions. Assumptions are guesses you make to bridge what you think with what you know. I'll give you an example. A colleague of mine, who is a master of team building, taught me that the most important question to ask a client who wants to do team building is, "why?" As with the payroll scenario, the temptation may be to jump at the bright lure of "team building" and sell the client a trust fall and a ropes course. But team building activities are often done in a superficial and ineffective way. A client typically believes they need team building when in reality there is a larger issue facing the people in the organization. Only by asking questions, listening carefully, and diagnosing accurately will you find the real root cause of the client's issue, and the most appropriate solution.

You've talked about the importance of diagnosing accurately. Can you tell me more about how to do that?

The general idea is to use the information your client is giving you to build a picture in your head of their situation, looking for patterns of symptoms that point to a problem you know how to solve. Imagine you are a doctor, and you are asking a sick patient to describe what's wrong. They start by saying "I have a sore throat." Important, but not sufficient for a diagnosis, right? A sore throat could indicate anything from the common cold to esophageal cancer. You need more information.

You'd ask questions to narrow down the possibilities. Does the patient have a stuffy nose? Other aches and pains? Recently swallowed liquid that was too hot? Do they smoke? There are lots of variables, but as you collect the answers to these questions, you get a more complete picture. You then compare that against your mental database of diseases, and come up with a diagnosis. We know from research and from the occasional unpleasant news headline that when doctors try to do this too quickly, they can get it wrong, sometimes with disastrous consequences for the patient. You wouldn't want your doctor to jump to a premature or inaccurate conclusion, and you shouldn't do it either. Take your time to make sure you really understand what your "patient" – your client – is telling you.

It can be helpful, as part of your pre-meeting preparation, to have a framework in mind for building that mental picture. For example, as a business coach, I might plug the different facts my client gives me into a "SLOT" analysis (strengths, limitations, opportunities and threats). Or I might use a tool called the "Balanced Scorecard," a four-quadrant model that examines the "voices" of the management, customer, supplier, and financial elements of the business. There are dozens of different frameworks you might use; pick one that fits your particular expertise and business model.

You and your client are each traveling a winding path in your businesses. The paths will intersect at various times, and to various degrees. Your goal is to create a map of the two routes, and discover the place where they run close and parallel for long enough that you'll both benefit by traveling together.

What if you don't have the right service for the client?

Don't be shy about walking away when you don't find a fit. You can make a loyal friend, and perhaps a future client, by proactively ending the conversation if you determine that your service is not a good fit for them at this time. Remember that you are a peer to your client, with expertise and value to bring to the table. You, who are an unquestionable expert in what you do, are uniquely positioned to help the client avoid buying services they don't need. Your goal is to create a mutually beneficial business relationship. Give your client the same advice you'd give any other trusted friend or colleague. They'll be incredibly grateful to you for your honesty, and for the time and money you have saved them.

Years ago, I worked in a bookstore. From time to time, a customer would come in looking for a book we did not have in stock. Of course, our first offer was to order the book for them. But if they needed it that day, we would call other bookstores in the neighborhood and do our best to find the book for the customer. Sometimes this meant the customer bought a book from one of our competitors. You can bet they came back to us, though, the next time they were shopping for books! This is one simple example of a very important principle. Be the client's "assistant buyer." Build trust, be on their agenda, and help them buy what they need, even when it doesn't happen to be something you're selling, and you will have a loyal customer and raving fan for life.

Those are certainly the kind of clients I would want. What if things are not going well in a sales meeting? How would I know that?

If the client was willing to meet with you in the first place, and you are asking thoughtful questions and staying on their agenda, you should be in good shape. That said, the client has to commit to five things before they will write you a check:

- They have to buy you. This one is the most critical — if they don't like you or aren't confident in your ability to solve their problem, you're done.
- They have to buy your company — your brand and your reputation.
- They have to buy the specific product or service under consideration.
- They have to accept your price.
- They have to be ready to start the relationship now.

Sometimes it's helpful to ask "test" questions. You could ask, "based on what we've discussed so far, if you had to make a purchase decision now, what would you say?" This kind of question shows you are sensitive to issues of fit with the client's needs and respect for the client's time. If the answer is "no," you may be able to ask what the client's concerns are and how you can address them satisfactorily, or you may be better off ending the conversation on a pleasant note, leaving an opening for a later meeting. Ask questions, rather than making statements. Questions make it very clear that you want to be on the client's agenda.

If the client is asking *you* a lot of questions, like "how do you work," "who have you worked with before," and "what's your hourly rate," you're either very close to a sale, or miles away from one. In a successful meeting, these are pro forma questions, asked at the end of the meeting, that help reassure the client that they are making a good choice and provide specifics for moving forward. In an unsuccessful meeting, these are questions asked at the beginning of the meeting, that help an uninterested person find an excuse to avoid speaking further with you about doing business. Often you can overcome these early objections by telling the client a bit more about yourself and your background, to develop rapport and establish yourself on a solid, equal professional footing with them.

Any last thoughts you would like to share?

A quick review of the key ideas:

- Get on the client's agenda and stay there. Remember to WAIT—ask yourself, "Why Am I Talking?" and take the shortest route back to listening mode.
- Show genuine respect and interest in your client, and seek the fit that creates mutual benefit.

- Remember that you are a professional of equal stature to anyone you meet. You bring tremendous value to every client interaction. You prove it by asking great questions, listening thoughtfully, diagnosing accurately, and demonstrating to the client how partnering with you will help them achieve the results they want.

By consistently applying these human principles to your selling process, you will become a trusted advisor to your clients, and a true selling genius!

Tracy Lunquist is a business advisor, leadership coach and professional facilitator, and the president of Working Magic. Tracy helps professional people use more of what they have to get more of what they want. By accurately diagnosing and addressing each client's unique needs, Tracy is able to help the owners of growing businesses achieve their goals and improve their results. A few of the tools Tracy uses in her process include evaluation, strategic planning, leadership development and time management coaching.

Years of experience in teaching, training and instructional design, as well as sales operations and product marketing, have helped Tracy hone her accessible writing style as well as her ability to build confidence in new leaders and small business owners. Her business and leadership articles have appeared in *Confident Women* magazine as well as her own blog and newsletter. She has spoken to numerous business and community groups including Rotary Clubs, Chambers of Commerce and chapters of Business and Professional Women and the American Business Women's Association.

Tracy is a member of the DeLand Area Chamber of Commerce, WOAMTEC (Women on a Mission to Earn Commission), and is president of the First Coast Chapter of Women in Aviation, International. Tracy holds a Master of Education degree from the University of Illinois at Urbana-Champaign, and is a member of the Honor Society of Phi Kappa Phi.

Tracy Lunquist

Working Magic
1113 S. Pearl St.
DeLand, Florida 32720
Phone: 386-736-5825
www.workingmagic.net
workwizard@workingmagic.net

CHAPTER SEVEN

Winning Formulas for Sales Presentations

Andre Boykin, Partner, *CAPITAL iDEA*

"When I am getting ready to reason with a man, I spend one-third of my time thinking about myself and what I am going to say and two-thirds about him and what he is going to say." —Abraham Lincoln

What principle of selling has helped you be consistently successful?

A great presentation is only a great presentation if it puts the prospect's needs first. A great presentation is a targeted presentation; one that is focused on what the customer will buy, and not on what the salesperson is trying to sell.

People buy on emotion and then justify the decision logically. A lot of sales people will tell you it is important to have the prospect "like" you. I agree. However the prospect will "like" me not because of how nice I am, or how well I can articulate the features of my products or services. A prospect will "like" me if they are convinced I am looking out for their best interests. When the prospect is thoroughly convinced I have their best interests in mind, they trust me. Trust is the foundation of the relationship between a sales person and a prospect. More trust, more sales.

People are prompted to take action and will take action quickly when they feel that action serves their best interests. Creating a presentation that proves you have taken the time to understand their needs will build the trust that leads to more sales.

What do you mean by the presentation phase of the sales process?

The presentation phase of the sales process falls in a sequence of steps that make up the sales process. There are six steps in total:

- **The Open** – This is the introductory part of the sales process where you are beginning to establish rapport with your prospect.
- **Establishing Credibility** – In this step you build trust with your prospect. You earn the right to continue to the next steps in the sales process.
- **Discovery** – This step is the most important in the sales process. Your goal is to learn as much as you can about your prospect. You want to understand their issues, needs, wants, goals and objectives, who are the buying influencers, decision making criteria, alternatives to be considered, and time frame for making a decision. This is just a partial list. The more you know, the better position you are in to serve your prospect.
- **Presentation** – You take what you learned in the discovery phase of the sales process and compellingly show how your solution will satisfy their needs and wants.
- **Agreement** – This is a natural outcome if you have done everything right up to this point! Sometimes this is called "closing a sale," but I prefer to think of it as opening a business relationship.
- **Implementation and Follow-up** – You put your solution into action, monitor the success, and remain in communication with your

customer. Always look for ways to increase your presence and do more business with your customer.

The important thing to understand is that there *is* a sales process. The presentation and proposal phase is a part of the process. There is a right time to do the presentation and proposal. Knowing when to make the presentation is just as important as the presentation itself!

What happens if you make the presentation prematurely in the sales process?

Most likely, you will not get the business. There is a definite progression in the sales process. The presentation and proposal phase comes after the discovery of needs and wants. If you make the presentation and proposal too early in the sales process, you're not going to have enough information or understanding about your prospect. How are you going to present if you don't understand your prospect's needs and wants? How do you know if what you intend to provide is what they want? You can never have too much information. A premature presentation in most cases means you have not gotten the information you need, and your presentation then becomes a generic "sales pitch" to the prospect.

Making the presentation prematurely is a very common occurrence. It seems in a sales situation we are so anxious to present because we feel that's where the action is. The real action comes in discovery. If you're able to discover your prospect's needs and wants, then you're going to be much more effective in giving a presentation. Asking the right questions and understanding the answers puts you in the "Winning Posture."

On the other hand, giving the presentation before you discover your prospect's needs and wants is a death sentence for your chances of getting the business. You want to give the presentation and proposal when it is time. The right time is when you have uncovered all of the needs and wants of your prospect so that you can recommend a unique solution for their specific situation.

What is Winning Posture? How does it come into play when preparing and giving a presentation?

Winning Posture is how you "show up" to others. Are you coming across in a way that's going to cause the other person to hear what you have to say and become associated with you? Winning Posture is "showing up" in a way that puts you in a position to win every time. There are three components of Winning Posture:

- **Your Mindset** – Be mindful of how you think about yourself, others, and your situation. Developing and exhibiting Winning Posture is the key to successful presenting. The mindset you want is total confidence--what you are presenting will benefit your prospect by addressing the needs they have expressed. You have to be confident, without question, that you have the best solution available.

- **Your Skills** – Have confidence in your ability to perform. You want to have the skills and be confident in your ability to present your solution in a compelling and persuasive manner. This includes your general presentation skills, and also your thorough preparation for each specific presentation you make.

- **Your Purpose and Goals** – Knowing your purpose or goal in making the presentation is vital. You want to be completely clear on the outcome you want to achieve. After all, when was the last time you just happened to achieve something? Without a goal or target, you are depending on luck to lead you in the right direction. Can you afford to leave your sales results to luck?

When you have these three things aligned perfectly, you are authentic and naturally attractive to others. How often have you heard someone say: "there is *something* about that person that makes me want to be associated with them?" That *something* is Winning Posture.

What type of environment do you want to create in a presentation meeting?

The best environment is one in which your prospect feels free to discuss what is occurring in his life or business. There are many ways of fostering this environment. Here are some thoughts about how to create it.

The presentation is really a dialogue. It's not an "I talk, you listen" kind of situation, and you don't want it to be that way. Ask open- ended questions throughout the presentation sales meeting. Open-ended questions begin with words like how, what, and why. Open-ended questions cause a dialogue to take place. For example, when you cover vital information in your presentation, you could ask: "How do you see this impacting your organization?" or, "Why do you think it will be important to implement this in your organization?" It is important to understand what your prospect is thinking and feeling. When your questions are open-ended, you invite your prospect to participate in a buying process that aligns with your selling process.

If you have the opportunity, invite your prospect to come to your location. This is absolutely the best way to control the environment and factors that impact the effectiveness of a presentation. In your office, you are familiar with the layout, you know what resources are available, and you can control interruptions. There is a lot to be said for having the "home field advantage!"

Because of technology, there are more options than ever for giving your presentation. Traditional methods for delivering a proposal are in person, by phone, by mail, or by e-mail. With tools such as WebEx and Go to Meeting, you can now deliver a presentation effectively via internet teleconference or videoconference. Regardless of the delivery method, you want to create an environment where all of the meeting participants can focus on the presentation. Keep the participants focused on the presentation by involving them in the conversation.

What do you want to avoid when delivering a presentation?

Don't deliver a proposal without a presentation. The proposal may be made by any of the means previously discussed, however delivering a proposal via mail, e-mail or by any other means without a presentation just simply doesn't work. I have been guilty of sending a proposal via e-mail without benefit of presentation. The results are always the same: I don't make the sale. We have been discussing the importance of an active dialogue with the prospect during a presentation. Obviously such a dialogue is impossible if you are not there to make the presentation. Don't send a proposal to your prospect until you have an appointment to present it. Without that appointment, it is wiser to assume they are not yet ready for the presentation phase, and you should be doing additional discovery.

Can you explain the sequence of steps during a presentation sales call?

We have previously discussed the sequence of steps in the sales process, and each effective sales call uses a very similar sequence of steps to be successful. No matter where you are in the sales process, follow these six steps. The six steps in a sales call are: Preparation, Open, Discovery, Present, Gain Agreement, and Implement. Let's look at each step to see what you want to accomplish in a presentation sales call.

Preparation – The call begins even before you are sitting in front of the client. If you have done your homework, you should have a clear understanding of who will attend the meeting. Be familiar with their position in the company, what they specifically do and what role they will play in the decision making process. In addition, ascertain the reason each person is attending the meeting. For instance, you may have been dealing with the CEO, but he has decided to bring his finance and operational people to the meeting. Rather than being blindsided, take the time to ask who will be there and the reasons they are there.

The Open – The purpose of the open is to establish rapport and set the pace for the meeting. Open the meeting by asking a simple question: "What are the best possible outcome for each of you in this meeting today?" You are asking them to express their expectations, and when they are encouraged to do that up front, your prospect feels involved and valued.

Discovery – Even at the presentation phase, your primary goal is to understand your prospect's wants and needs. Businesses are dynamic by nature, so ask: has anything changed since the last time you met with them? This is very important! To illustrate how important it is to ask this question, a few years ago, I had a meeting with the president of a property management company. I had my presentation, based on my fact finding, to propose a leadership development process for some of the leaders in the organization. After opening the call and establishing rapport with the meeting participants, I asked: "Has anything changed since the last time I was here?"

Out of the conversation that ensued, I found that the organization was headed in a totally different direction in the development of the leaders. I didn't even pull out my proposal that I had prepared. Instead, I went back into "discovery" mode, asking questions about their new direction. If I had not asked the initial question and proceeded with my original proposal, I would have wasted everyone's time. After gathering more information, I was able to come back with a new proposal that secured a much larger project with the company.

Presentation – Present your solution in a compelling way. Presenting in a compelling manner means delivering your information with conviction and excitement. Come to the meeting well-prepared. Remember to keep everyone involved by using open-ended questions to draw out thoughts and feelings. Most people don't really listen to what you are saying. They are really listening to *themselves* talking about what you are saying. It's your job to make sure everyone is understanding your presentation the way you mean for it to be understood.

Gain Agreement – Invite your prospect to agree to move to the next step. The next step could be to formulate an agreement to do business, provide more information, or start a trial program. The idea is to move the sale forward and closer to the goal of securing the business.

Implement – Put into action whatever you gained agreement on. Outline and explain the next steps. Be sure to set a date and time for the next steps to be implemented.

What elements make a good presentation? In other words, what should you include in the presentation?

You want the presentation to look sharp. Any printed material should be bound, not stapled, and should be printed on quality paper. Your audience will begin to judge you the moment you initially distribute the presentation. You want your presentation to convey that you are worthy to do business with them.

A quality presentation has to have great content. The specifics may vary according to your industry, but there are some "must haves" that you absolutely have to include in your proposal. Let's look at what those are.

Begin with a section that outlines the facts uncovered in your discovery phase of the sales process. Outlining what you have learned about the organization shows that you understand the prospect's needs, goals and objectives. This section can be in bullet or list form, or it can be written in paragraphs. If you demonstrate your knowledge of the organization, it demonstrates you understand what impact your solution will have on the organization. This section sets the stage for conveying your solution from a position of being an "insider."

The next section in your presentation is the solution. Always think about the goods and services that you're providing as a solution to a problem your prospect has. In the solution section reveal what your solution is and compellingly show how it resolves your prospect's issues. You want to showcase not only the "what" of your solution, but also the "how."

It is very easy to focus on the features which are the "what" and "how" when presenting the solution, and at some point the details will be important to discuss. To be more effective, though, focus on benefits and the return on investment your solution provides. Simply stated, benefits are what the features actually mean to your prospect.

For example, a fast turnaround time is a feature. Fast turnaround time allows your prospect to provide faster service to their clients. Better service means higher productivity and greater profits. The benefit to your client is more money in their pocket. Prospects must clearly understand what the bottom line impact of fast turnaround means to them. Don't leave it up to the prospect to "figure it out." Show them. Say "What this means to you is...." Making this statement is a surefire way to know you are talking about benefits and not features. Your bottom line for more sales is to make sure you don't forget your prospect's bottom line.

Finally, deliver a summary that combines all of the pieces of your solution, in one page or less. This is when you have a chance to gauge commitment and find out if you have made a sale.

How should you handle presenting the price of your products or services in a proposal?

Keep the investment for your services out of the presentation until you have agreement from your prospect that what you have proposed is what they want. Allow me to illustrate. Early on in my sales career, I was selling truck leasing and logistic services. I called on a food distributor and I had put together a really nice proposal for my prospect. The first thing he did when I gave him the presentation was to go to the back page to see the investment for my service. When he looked at that page, his eyes got big, and he said, "I can't believe it's this much." He did allow me to go through my presentation. However the whole time I was going through the presentation I was fighting to justify the investment for the service. I didn't get the business.

Over the next several months I kept in touch with him and kept calling on him. In time, I came back with another presentation and this time I left the investment for my services out of the proposal. I said, "Let's walk through this presentation and have a conversation about our services and what they could mean to you." He immediately went to the back page and was thumbing through the presentation. I asked, "What are you looking for?" He said, "I'm looking for how much it is." I said, "You won't find it. We're going to have a discussion about how our solution will satisfy your needs; then we'll talk about the investment." He said, "Okay." I went through the presentation and asked him if this met his needs. He said it did. I walked out of that presentation with a signed agreement. Don't reveal the investment for your service until your prospect has reviewed your solution and agreed that it is what they want.

What is a unique value proposition, and why is having a unique value proposition so important?

Let's first take a look at what value really is. The definition of value is the benefit of the product or service that one provides minus the cost. Your unique value proposition is the benefit or value that only you can bring to the prospect. On the surface you might say there is no such thing as unique value. But there really is. If nothing else, they get *you*, and believe me, *you* are unique.

Uniqueness can come in the form of methodology, systems, processes, experience, or special knowledge. Any number of things could make your solution unique. The key is to understand thoroughly the features and benefits of your products or services in comparison to the alternatives that are available to your prospect. Without a unique value proposition your solution is the same as everyone else's.

If two alternatives are equal, the only thing left to compare is the investment for service because you are a commodity. Your presentation needs to pass the "white-out" test. If you're able to take your name and "white it out" and replace it with the name of a competitor, then your proposal has failed the "white-out" test. When you fail the "white-out" test, you are really saying to your prospect: "We do the same thing for everybody. You are not special."

You want to bring a unique value proposition to this particular prospect, and the only way to do that is to have a clear understanding of the client's needs and wants. That's why the discovery part of the sales process is so vital to being effective in the presentation stage.

How does a presentation overcome objections?

Objections may be a natural part of the sales process, but they don't need to be. If you have taken the time to discover all of the prospect's wants and needs up front, you should have addressed any objections in the proposal and subsequent presentation. If you know something is going to be an issue with the prospect, then why not bring it up? If you wait for your prospect to make an objection, you risk becoming adversarial. Better to address their concerns proactively, and demonstrate that you are looking out for their interests.

Let me give you an illustration. Let's say that you're getting hit over and over again with the same objection about the timeliness of your delivery. In your presentation, you could talk about timeliness of delivery and say: "In some cases our prospects have raised concerns about our timeliness of delivery. After looking at the total picture what they found out was... and we were able to earn the right to do business with them." Then follow with: "How do you see that impacting your organization?" That way you've covered a potential objection in the presentation. You have cleared it up on your timetable and in the way you want to present the issue. Why wait until the end of the presentation when ideally you want to be talking about the next steps? By discussing it during the presentation, even if it was not a concern with your prospect, it is handled and out of the way.

In some cases, proposals need to be viewed by others in the organization before a decision is made. How should you handle this situation?

Buying influencers are people in the organization who will have a say in whether or not you're going to do business with that organization. There is only one person who has the ability to say yes and deliver the funds for your goods and services; that person is the Decision Maker. However, there are other influencers. These include the person(s) who actually use the product or service. These are Users. There are also people who evaluate your product or service. These Analyzers can say no to your product or service, but they can't say yes. Examples of analyzers are CPAs, attorneys, and CFOs. Their role in the buying process is to ensure that the integrity of the organization's criteria for making purchasing decisions is kept. Analyzers often confer with the decision maker as an advisor. Analyzers can be inside the organization (employees) or outside the organization (contractors, consultants, etc.).

You want to make sure you understand who the buying influencers are and how they are going to be involved in the decision making process. That way you can tailor your presentation to meet each of their needs. In the discovery process, ask questions about who the influencers might be. Ask to meet with them to discuss their issues. Include their issues in the proposal and address them in your presentation to the decision maker.

What buying signals should you be looking for in the presentation?

You want to see people nodding their heads and being positive in their conversations. When people are nodding their heads in agreement, and smiling, that's an indication that they're right with you. That's one of the buying signals you're looking for. Before anyone buys, they have to connect with you!

If you see your prospect projecting themselves into the future with your solution, that is a good sign. For example, if your prospect asks: "When we implement this solution do we have to....?" The prospect is already imagining your solution in place. Or they might say: "I like the fact that when we have this solution we will be able to... " This kind of projection is a very strong buying signal. When this happens you may not even need to complete your presentation because they're ready to do business with you. If they're ready to do business with you, you can always go over the missed pieces of the presentation at a later date. Always be aware of indications the prospect is ready to move forward with you and take immediate action if that is the case.

One time, I was making a presentation with a great prospect. We had built a good working relationship together. The prospect asked me, "What do I do now?" What I should have said was, "Well, the only thing left for us to do is get started." Instead I went back to giving the prospect more information. I had failed to realize the prospect was ready to get started on the solution. I did not recognize the buying signal and lost the business. Ouch! Be in tune and listen to what they say. Just as importantly, listen to what is not being said. Listen for the experience behind what they're saying.

Do you have any closing thoughts for our readers?

Learn all you can about your prospect. Understand their style, their motivations and their reasons for buying. Make no assumptions.

Presentation excellence takes practice. Implement the formulas outlined here by practicing them over and over again until they become habitual. Know the steps in the sales process and the steps of a sales call so well that you do them without thinking about it. Practice the questions that you will ask in the presentation. Visualize how you will create the best environment possible to give your presentation.

After each presentation, critique yourself. Ask yourself what happened? What could I have done better? What did I do well that I want to continue to do? It's a good idea whether you get the business or not to ask your prospect why they chose to do or not do business with you.

Practice, have fun, and continue to learn and improve. Happy Selling!

Andre Boykin has over twenty-five years' experience working with organizations to help them maximize their performance. His purpose in life is to help others use more of their potential in their daily lives. Andre is an accomplished speaker, lecturer, facilitator, and trainer and has the ability to reach his audience and move people to action.

In 2002, Andre and his partner, Shari Roth, formed CAPITAL iDEA, a firm that works with organizations to create environments where employees are engaged, valued, and empowered to achieve outstanding results. Together, Andre and Shari have worked with leaders and sales teams in distribution, consumer package goods, health care, construction, insurance, finance, and hospitality. Andre has been featured in numerous local and national publications on topics of sales and leadership.

Andre is a certified Behavioral and Workplace Motivators Analyst and certified to administer the Hartman Value Profile

Andre Boykin

CAPITAL iDEA
2090 Augusta
Weston, Florida
954-349-5828
www.capital-idea.net
www.andreboykin.com
andre@andreboykin.com

CHAPTER EIGHT

Be True to Yourself: You Don't Have to Sell to Sell

Rick Kolster, Managing Director, *Peak Performance Development*

"The man who lives for himself is a failure; the man who lives for others has achieved true success." —Norman Vincent Peale

What principle of selling has helped you be consistently successful?

Have a purpose and be passionate about it, whatever that purpose is. It should be what gets you up in the morning and what keeps you driving all day. It is what defines who you are to your customers and your prospects. It is your motivation to sell and your prospect's motivation to buy. Defining your purpose helps you build the attitudes you will need to be successful.

Knowing your purpose enables you to begin each day focused and clear. You need to know what you want and then go after it with rifle shot intensity and pinpoint accuracy. When you are congruent with your purpose, it is much easier to love what you do and be really good at it. From personal experience, I found early in my career that I needed to turn my vocation into my avocation to be truly effective.

Having a clear purpose allows you to work in a purposeful manner. So many people really don't enjoy what they do and just keep doing it anyway! In my experience there are three kinds of people in the world. The first are people who have no idea what they want to do or what their purpose is. They are frustrated and bounce from task to task, job to job, situation to situation and never succeed at anything. The second are those who only do what they must. They must get married, get a job, have kids, go to church – only because they must. They may appear successful, but they are usually not very happy. The third type have purpose and do what they want to do. They are fulfilled.

Those business owners and sales people that fall into the third category are the ones who sell without selling. Because they are congruent with their purpose and know how to communicate it, they are able to communicate on a base level with prospects and clients. They are authentic.

Ask yourself how you rate. If you are struggling with your sales efforts, perhaps it is not about your sales abilities. Perhaps it is about your lack of purpose. Remember that one definition of insanity is doing the same thing again and again and expecting to love your job more. Okay, so that's not exactly the definition as it has been quoted, but it is more to the point.

Why is purpose so important?

In the movie *Jerry McGuire*, Rod Tidwell, played by Cuba Gooding Jr., talks to Jerry about his "Quan". His "Quan" was his purpose. The phrase we all remember from the movie is *"SHOW ME THE MONEY."* It's a catchy saying, but it is not what the movie is about. It is really about purpose. Rod's purpose was to provide his family with a better life than he grew up with. He lived his whole life to create opportunities for them to be anything they could be. That was his "Quan", or his purpose. What is yours?

In your sales role, you surely want customers to "show you the money." But why? It's probably not just so you can have a thick stack of green pieces of paper in your wallet. Your purpose completes you – it's where "show me the money" meets the life you mean to build with it. Success in sales by itself will not make you happy, and the idea of success in sales by itself probably doesn't motivate you much. So what *would* make you happy? What does your perfect life look like? When you know that, you will know your purpose and you will find your motivation.

What do you mean when you say you don't have to sell to sell?

Selling gets such a bad rap. Most of the time the words "sales" or "selling" conjure up negative visuals and emotions. For you as a business owner or professional who is known as an expert in something else, just imagining you have to sell can paralyze you.

The truth is, you really don't have to sell to sell. Think of selling in a different way. Selling is about helping your prospect make a good buying decision. To do so, you must create a relationship based on the truth. The truth is being congruent with your purpose. It is about believing in yourself and your product.

Have you ever been asked: "Go ahead, give me your sales pitch"? When asked, what is your first inclination? If you are like most people, you want to answer right away with your best line. Since you have been practicing your elevator speech, aren't you just waiting to be asked? Doesn't it feel great when you nail it? Do you usually get the business, or do you get something like this: "Oh, that's...nice."

I don't have a sales pitch. I have no idea what my prospective client wants to hear. I don't know because I haven't found out what's important to them. My purpose is to help my prospects make the right decision and to do so, I must be a trusted advisor to them.

To demonstrate the client side of the equation, think about how you go about buying. Do you wake up and think, " HMMMM, I think I'm going to let someone sell me something today"? Probably not. It just doesn't happen. Alternatively, I bet there have been days when you thought, "Gee, I sure would like to go and buy something today." (I do have daughters.)

People don't like to be sold, but they love to buy. Buying satisfies a perceived need or want. The purchase may be a necessity, a luxury, a reward or a solution to a problem. In some cases the need hasn't yet been defined. There is no value in the purchase because no value has been translated from the perceived need or want. If you are selling without selling, you are acting as a value translator for your client. When you do that, your client can make the right buying decision.

Conversely, have you ever felt tricked, manipulated or sold? Have you ever felt after the fact that you have been talked into making a purchase you really didn't want? When you got back home or to the office after making the purchase, how did you feel? If you're like most people, at best you felt bad about the purchase, and at worst you felt bad about yourself. And as for how you felt about the sales person, I doubt you would want a customer of yours ever to feel that way about you!

This is the difference between helping your prospect buy, and "selling" them. When you help someone buy, you create mutual respect and trust. You foster a good relationship. When you "sell" your prospect, the door is left wide open to buyer's remorse, regret and little chance of any further relationship. The best strategy for the business professional who has to generate revenue is simple: help your prospect make a good buying decision. Then you will be selling without selling.

Why do people buy?

There are many reasons why people buy. When people perceive a need, they may have an initial reason. Impulse purchases fall into this category. The buyer has an impulse to buy, and will generally listen to just about any pitch. They will allow the person selling to give them their reasons to buy. Salespeople who only want to make one sale will happily feed the buying impulse and a sale will be made. There is a high risk of buyer's remorse in this transaction, but the salesperson may not care. If there is no need to interact with the client again it doesn't matter. The salesperson can get away with telling their prospects what they want to hear.

For most readers of this book, however, a one-time sale is not enough to build a sustainable business. It is important for your clients to *continue* to buy. For example, why do you go back to the same restaurant? Why do you continue to use the services of your CPA? Why do you continue to go back to the same store to buy new products? You continue to buy because you are satisfied with the product or service you have purchased and have created a relationship with the business. Without a reason to change, you will continue to eat in the same restaurant, have your taxes done by the same CPA and shop in the same store. You might continue as a customer even if their prices are higher than those of their competitors.

Why do people buy higher priced goods or services? Doesn't a sale always come down to price?

Price is only important in the absence of value. As we discussed earlier, if you are helping your customers to buy, you are translating the value of your goods or services into terms your prospect will understand. When you understand what your prospect will buy, when they will buy, how they will buy and for what reasons they will buy, you are in a position to build value. Value is not price sensitive.

As an expert in your field, you bring unique value to your customer. A big part of that unique value is your ability to understand the customer's needs and help them make the right buying decisions. When you demonstrate this by being true to yourself and true to your purpose, you'll deliver value far beyond any price you could charge for your services.

"Be True to Yourself" is the title of your chapter. Could you say more about that?

Being true to yourself means being true to your purpose. It is a foundational concept for business leaders who need to generate revenue. Far too often we make promises that we can't fulfill. My dad had a saying: *"Don't let your alligator mouth get your hummingbird behind in trouble."* We try to tell the prospect or the customer in front of us things they might want to hear, as opposed to what's really true.

Have you had the experience of working with a salesperson or service organization that over-promises and under-delivers? How do you feel when that happens? Is this the kind of experience you want your clients to have?

When you are true to yourself, you make promises to your customers that you know you can keep. Being true to yourself means that you have a realistic understanding of the results you can deliver and the levels of service you truly can provide. If you are unclear about your service delivery or results, you will over-promise. Even though you may exert a lot of time and effort living up to your promises, it is likely that you will fall short of customer expectations. You have been incongruent, and have under-delivered.

Under-delivery comes from telling your customer what they want to hear. Perhaps you have fallen into this trap. Have you heard yourself:

- Promise you will always be available although you know customers often have difficulty reaching you?
- Promise regular follow-up when you struggle with follow-up?
- Promise services or capabilities you do not yet know how to deliver?
- Promise a delivery timeline that is unrealistic?
- Promise a level of quality that you know you have never reached?

Under-delivery shows a lack of respect for your customer and a lack of respect for yourself. You are not being honest with yourself or the people you want to do business with. Telling people what they want to hear is short-sighted at best and harmful or dangerous at worst.

Overselling is akin to over-promising. How many times have you seen salespeople that "show up and throw up?" When you oversell it is generally because you need to make the sale more than your client needs to buy. It signals desperation to your prospect. You are putting so much energy into having your prospect "bend to your will" that they feel strong-armed and you lose the sale. This particular approach only yields short-term gain. You pay for it with long-term negative consequences. When we oversell we just throw everything out on the table. We verbally throw up all over the prospect. It can be really MESSY STUFF.

Overselling is telling your prospect all about your wonderful product or service without asking them if it is right for them. You are making their decisions for them. You may even sell past the close! You may talk your client out of buying from you! We get so excited about making a sale, and so proud of what we do that we keep selling, we keep talking. Is that the way you like to buy? Why would you think that others want to buy that way from you?

Selling past the sale is a symptom of incongruence. You are not being true to yourself. You aren't listening or paying attention. More deals are blown because of overselling than for any other reason. When you are congruent with your principles and true to yourself you will always be delivering more than the customer expects.

How does this affect your success as a sales person?

The outcome of congruence is a long-term sale and/or a repeat customer. Being true to yourself is core. It is much easier to do more business with a current client than it is to get a new one. When we meet the customer's needs and solve their problems, we build loyalty. Isn't that the point? You have other things to do besides sell, don't you? The time spent keeping existing clients is bound to be much more valuable than the time spent getting new ones.

People buy from someone they know, like, and trust. Become that company or individual that people know, like, and trust, and your repeat business will increase dramatically – and so will your profits. The existing customer knows you, knows what you can and will do, and has built a level of trust and familiarity with you. For your customer, the choice is easy. They will be much more likely to buy from you every time.

Why do non-sales professionals fall into the over promise/under deliver trap?

The number one reason we fall into the trap is desperation. I mentioned it before, but it bears repeating. We become desperate to close the sale. We've got external and internal pressures to satisfy our own needs and close a deal. We've got bills to pay, payroll, current customers to satisfy and employees to mentor and counsel. Some people may even doubt that they can actually do the work. They doubt the abilities of the people who work for them. They don't believe in the quality they provide. They have no purpose.

What happens when sales people don't believe in themselves?

They rely on "techniques" from many years ago. The way many people were taught to sell just don't work anymore. Old-school selling relies on "techniques." Techniques are often manipulative ways to get the customer to buy. Today's buyers are much more sophisticated though. They can see a pitch coming before it even gets to them, and it puts them on alert. Techniques create resistance, and resistance gets in the way of selling. *Techniques don't sell.*

I've been selling for more than 25 years, and as a young salesman I learned all the "sure fire closing statements" that were taught by the so-called "masters of sales". I was taught that if I used these techniques I would close a higher percentage of my deals. The old maxim was: "Selling is just a numbers game." If I see a greater number of prospects, use the "sure fire" techniques, and "ABC" (Always Be Closing), I would exceed my quota and get rich from the commissions.

Let me give you a few examples of classic techniques. The Puppy Dog Close preys on your attachment to a product if you take it home you will love it. The Door Handle Close relies on the last minute appeal and the last minute "special deal". The Colombo Close asks dumb questions so you will incriminate yourself into a sale. The Ben Franklin Close has you prepare a list of pros and cons for comparison purposes – and of course, the pros always win! The Take Away Close actually threatens the buyer – better buy now or you'll never be able to get this great deal again.

When you describe the techniques like this, they sound a little crazy, don't they? Today's buyers are smarter than that. They have the opportunity to access the internet to find out about your product or service before you even walk in the door. They have looked at your competition, made comparisons and are just waiting for you to make claims about what you do. If you aren't congruent with your purpose, or if you sell in a manner that is untrue to yourself, you will be shown the door. No technique in this world will cover for overselling, over-promising, or incongruence with your purpose. If you can afford to go hungry while you prove me right, feel free to try as many of those old techniques as you want.

The "trick" to success in sales is no trick – it's congruence with your purpose. You must believe in yourself in order to help your clients buy. You don't "close the deal", you help the client make the best decision about what to buy. Help them decide, even if the decision is to buy from someone else. When you are willing to let the sale go so that the customer will get what they really need, you are congruent. When you can put yourself in their shoes and look out for their interests, you will be headed down the right path.

How can you tell when you're headed down the *wrong* path?

Watch your customer and pick up on his or her physical clues or body language. Make it a point to pay attention. When your customer is talking about feelings or attitudes, 55 percent of their communication is in their body language. About 38 percent is tone of voice, and only seven percent are the words they are using. If the non-verbal seems like it's in conflict with the verbal message, the non-verbal message is more likely to reflect what they're really feeling. Your prospect is engaged if they're answering your questions and are trying to help you build a relationship with them.

The moment they begin to check their emails, look at their watch, doodle or pretend to read your proposal they are disengaged. You know you're headed down the wrong path. Remember your old friend, desperation? You get the lump in your throat, breathing becomes quicker, your palms sweat and you see the sale going away.

This is when those pesky old techniques start to sneak back, and you become tempted to use them again. The customer will RUN if you use them. When they start running, we start chasing. The more we chase, the more they become afraid, and fear in a customer is never good. Don't give in. Stay true to yourself.

How does fear factor into the sales process?

Fear plays on both sides of the sales equation. Everyone has experienced fear of some type at one time or another. It can be unnerving, debilitating, and downright paralyzing sometimes. For you as the seller, the fear may take the form of "Will I be able to pay this month's bills?", "Will I lose my business?", "Am I going to be able to feed my family?", or ultimately, "Will I survive?" For your prospect, fear of the fallout from making the wrong decision tops the list. Fear will stifle all creativity and lead us to make major mistakes even though we should know better.

There are three types of fear that play into the transaction: fear of change; fear of the unknown; and fear of failure.

Fear of the Unknown is the reason you get out of the bed in the middle of the night and go trekking around the house in your underwear with a baseball bat. You don't have a clue what you are afraid of. It is unreasoning, blind and debilitating if you let it be. We tend to worry with this fear, thinking excessively about something that hasn't happened, probably won't happen and is beyond our control anyway.

Fear of Change is very similar to the fear of the unknown. Most people think more about what is going to go wrong than what is going to go right, don't they? Fear of change is the fear that comes from self-defeating beliefs – believing that any change must be bad, or that the need for change means you are somehow a bad or inadequate person.

Fear of Failure is the most common fear. It is driven by all of the self-limiting beliefs we have about our ability and ourselves. It is the fear of having to tell someone close to us that we didn't do what we set out to do. Disappointment and despair are the fruits of the fear of failure.

When you are operating within your purpose, and are true to yourself, you dramatically reduce your fear. When you reduce your fear, you are able to ask the right questions of your prospect. When you ask the right questions, your prospect has the chance to answer. When your prospect answers, they are able to verbalize their fears and create their own solutions. Their fear is reduced. When their fear is reduced, their ability to make the right buying decision is increased. When they can make a good buying decision, you are more likely to make a sale.

How can I close more opportunities?

Your number one goal in any sales situation should be to help your client. The more successful you are in doing so, the more successful you will be in closing more business. In this context, helping your prospects means helping them make the right decisions for their businesses, their families and their lives. Keep your focus on the needs of your prospective customer to understand how you can best help them.

If your most important objective is to make the sale, you will tend to see your client as an object. Objects become obstacles, getting in the way of your objective. Objects don't have feelings or desires, and they are not unique or intelligent. They are lifeless. When the object doesn't do what you want it to do, negative feelings start to build in you. You feel annoyed, angry, frustrated, helpless or perhaps desperate. You push even harder.

When you view your client as a person with unique needs, feelings and desires the sale becomes different. It becomes client focused, not focused on you. People buy from you when they know you, like you, and trust you. There is a greater likelihood that this will be the case when they know you see them as a person and not just a number on your way to achieving your objective.

How do you change your attitude to overcome fear and have the confidence to make a sale?

Developing yourself to your fullest potential is the first step. Take the time to be an expert. Pre-call planning is critical; map out each call you make in advance. As Stephen Covey put it, *"Begin with the end in mind."* Know what your minimum acceptable outcome is. Have a clear definition for what you hope to accomplish during each call.

Know, like and trust yourself. Be the kind of person that you would like to buy from. Becoming that person begins with identifying and understanding your basic belief system. You've got to believe in your product or service. You have to have confidence that your product, or the service you provide, is going to be able to do exactly what you say it's going to do. Have confidence in what you do, who you are, the company you represent, and the service you provide. Confidence will help you overcome the fear. You've got to have some goals, and you've got to know what you want to accomplish before you go in.

Take 5 to 10 minutes right before a meeting to decide what you want to accomplish. Decide your best-case outcome, but think about the worst case as well. Is your objective another meeting, an introduction to another decision maker, or simply getting a piece of information that is missing?

If you are not able to accomplish your minimum acceptable outcome, decide if this is the right fit for you. Not all opportunities are the right ones. Not all opportunities will be congruent with your values and beliefs. Sometimes the best deals you do are the ones you walk away from. You may have read SWSWN in an earlier chapter. I have one more SW... SWSWSWN. Some Will. Some Won't. *So What?* Next! Move on to your next best prospect.

What attitudes or skills need to be developed to become more successful in sales?

Listening – we're born with two ears and one mouth, and I believe that there is a reason for that. We need to use these in the same ratio as we have them; we should be listening twice as much as we speak in any situation. In a sales situation this is even more critical. When you listen, you are putting the emphasis on your prospect, where it belongs. The sales process is not about your needs, it is about your prospect's needs.

Time Management – are you using the time you have allotted to selling as effectively as possible? Do you have a plan for your day? What activities support your purpose? How do your goals fit your purpose, and what progress are you making towards achieving them? The old adage goes: "People don't plan to fail, they just fail to plan." Are you planning your daily sales efforts on purpose?

Confidence – confidence is knowing that you are going to be able to do what you say you're going to do. It is not over-promising and under-delivering. Confidence shows when you under-promise and over-deliver.

What about when you're in front of the customer? What should go through your mind so you can build the relationship and complete the sale?

What's in it for them? What are they thinking? What do they want to get out of their end of the deal? Every person in every sales conversation is asking himself or herself the WIIFM question. To make the deal, we've got to help them answer their WIIFM question.

What does WIIFM mean in relation to getting a sale?

WIIFM, *What's In It For Me?* Your client is asking himself or herself how they will benefit from doing business with you. They expect you to be thinking the same thing about your end of the deal. If it is true that both of you are focused on "me," then the sales transaction will likely be an adversarial process. One of you will have to win, and one of you will lose. Turn the tables. If we're able to answer the "What's in it for me?" question for the customer, they're more likely to buy. If they're still scratching their heads and they're not sure how this is going to benefit them, they're more than likely not going to buy.

A boss of mine from years ago used to say: "A confused customer will not make a decision." When we are clear about what we can do and what we are selling, the customer can make a quick decision because we have helped them understand what they want and how we can get it for them. However if you are confused about what you're selling, so is your customer! They will do nothing. We want to have clarity, we want to give them clarity and tell them what is in it for them.

Do you have any final thoughts for our readers?

Selling without selling is about being true to yourself and your purpose. It's all about the little things you do that support the big thing, your purpose. Your purpose must include understanding what the customer needs. It is caring about what is best for the customer. It is helping them to make the best decision to get what they want.

Selling is not one big thing; it's the little things that you do. It's paying attention to people, it's caring about people, it's being true to yourself. Don't just sell; help them. Focus on that customer in front of you and not on yourself. See them as a person, not as an object or a number.

If you love what you do and you do it well, you will be well compensated for doing it. When your avocation becomes your vocation, you will be living the successful life we all dream about – doing what you love and loving what you do...on purpose.

Finally you've got to believe. Believe in your product or service, believe in your customer, and most importantly, believe in yourself. Know your purpose and believe in it, and you will succeed.

Coach Rick Kolster is a Certified Business Coach and Managing Director of Peak Performance Development. He and his company work with leaders and their organizations to increase their bottom line through personal and professional development.

Rick has over 28 years of business experience in numerous industries, ranging from restaurant and hospitality services to industrial sales and manufacturing. He is an expert in facilitating communication, sales, interpersonal skills and motivational development processes. While working primarily with the leadership of the organization, he has worked with all levels of client organizations. He works throughout the United States and Canada. Clients respect his ability to work with them to achieve measurable improvements in their results.

Rick's thinking style assists companies to recognize their existing paradigms in order to solve stubborn problems and work through challenging situations. He understands the critical difference between "training sessions" and the true development of a company's most important assets – its people.

Rick Kolster
Peak Performance Development
P.O. Box 92891
Southlake, TX 76092
817-748-7425
www.mypotentialplus.com
rick@mypotentialplus.com